BRIGHT I

THE AMERICAN BY HENRY JAMES

Intelligent Education

Nashville, Tennessee

BRIGHT NOTES: The American
www.BrightNotes.com

No part of this publication may be used or reproduced in any manner whatsoever without written permission, except in the case of brief quotations in critical articles and reviews. For permissions, contact Influence Publishers http://www.influencepublishers.com.

ISBN: 978-1-645421-92-4 (Paperback)
ISBN: 978-1-645421-93-1 (eBook)

Published in accordance with the U.S. Copyright Office Orphan Works and Mass Digitization report of the register of copyrights, June 2015.

Originally published by Monarch Press.
Vartkis Kinoian, 1965
2020 Edition published by Influence Publishers.

Interior design by Lapiz Digital Services. Cover Design by Thinkpen Designs.

Printed in the United States of America.

Library of Congress Cataloging-in-Publication Data forthcoming.
Names: Intelligent Education
Title: BRIGHT NOTES: The American
Subject: STU004000 STUDY AIDS / Book Notes

CONTENTS

1)	Introduction to Henry James	1
2)	Introduction to The American	11
3)	Textual Analysis	
	Chapter 1 - 5	18
	Chapters 6 - 10	35
	Chapters 11 - 15	49
	Chapters 16 - 20	63
	Chapters 21 - 26	78
4)	Character Analyses	91
5)	Critical Commentary	98
6)	Essay Questions and Answers	104
7)	Selected Bibliography	110

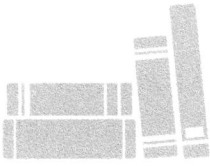

INTRODUCTION TO HENRY JAMES

LIFE (1843 - 1916)

Henry James is probably the outstanding American novelist and stylist. If he is not alone in that rank, he is accompanied by only three or four others, such as Hawthorne, Melville, Twain, and perhaps Faulkner. Even among those, who represent the best in American literature so far as novelists are concerned, James does seem to stand out if only on the basis of his prodigious lifetime of writing. James's writing career extended from the late 1860s to the first two decades of the present century, and he was without question the first American novelist to truly bring his work into the mainstream of world literature. This is not to say that there were not great works in American literature before James's major novels, but it is to say that James made the American novel something more than the product of an American. He made it an art form, a work as sophisticated as the well-written poem, and his works rank with the outstanding writers not only of America, but also of Europe.

The facts of James's life are best seen in relation to his work, for James lived a quiet life and devoted himself to literature as a profession and as a way of life. The following is a brief summary of some of the important dates, but the next section ("Periods in James's fiction") views James's works as the primary material for understanding him. The student should know at least the following: Henry James was born on April 15, 1843, in a house on Washington Square in New York City. James in his autobiography later told of the impressions he had of life because of the humanity he would observe in that respectable section of the great city. Henry's father, Henry James, Senior, was a well-known figure in intellectual circles. He had inherited his wealth and spent much of his time in cultured activity. The novelist's older brother, William, became famous as a philosopher, psychologist, and professor at Harvard University, and the brothers remained close, as their correspondence shows, throughout their lifetimes. Henry James, Senior, believed that his children should be exposed to the culture and life of Europe as a basic part of their life, so he took his sons there when Henry was still an infant. On their return from their first trip, they lived in New York again, but also stayed in Albany. In 1855 they returned to Europe again for three more years of education, some in school, some at the direction of tutors, and some led by the father, in Geneva, London, and Paris. During 1858-1859 the family stayed in Newport, Rhode Island, a very fashionable resort at that time, where Henry and William studied painting with John LaFarge, a well-known artist. In 1859-1860, however, they were in Europe again, this time in Geneva and also Bonn, Germany. In 1862, James entered the Law School at Harvard, while William entered the scientific school at the same university. In that same year, Henry sustained some mysterious injury to his back that kept him out of the Civil War. Around 1865 James began publishing his sketches, critical reviews, and stories, in such magazines as the famous *Atlantic Monthly* and the *North American Review*. It was just a year before this time that the young Henry James had decided on writing as his profession. The student should understand that James's decision was not an idealistic, romantic outburst, but a reasoned and mature commitment to writing as a career. In 1869 James went to Europe, and although he returned to America on several occasions, one can say that from that year on James was a resident of the European continent. Most students of American literature see James's expatriation as a pilgrimage in reverse of the normal pattern; it was a move, one must understand, made by an artist in order to give himself the proper perspective from which he could continue with his craft. James lived for the most part in London, but he spent some time in Paris, Rome, and other European cities. In 1915, although he was unmistakably an American in thought and art, James became a British subject in protest of American neutrality during that time of the First World War. James died in February, 1916.

PERIODS IN JAMES'S FICTION

Much more complete a view of James as a writer comes from looking at the stages in his long and fruitful writing career. F. W. Dupee in *Henry James* breaks that career into the following periods:

1. 1870s: This is James's idealistic phase. He is learning his craft and developing his themes. The works are really not complicated and characters are clearly drawn without too much ambiguity or complexity. Still James achieved in this early period some of his most memorable characters, such as Christopher Newman in *The American* (1877) and Isabel Archer in *The Portrait of a Lady* (1881). Other important early works are *Daisy Miller*, 1879; *The Europeans*, 1878; and *Washington Square*, 1881.

2. 1880s: James in this period became more realistic. He began to deal with more complicated matters such as

social institutions and political issues. Some important works are *The Princess Casamassima*, 1885; *The Bostonians*, 1886; and *The Tragic Muse*, 1887.

3. Late 1880s and Early 1890s: At this point, James turned to writing for the theatre with noticeably bad luck. He was humiliated on the night of the opening of his play *Gum Domville*, when the audience was vile to him. An interesting note is that a young critic, George Bernard Shaw, was at that performance.

4. 1890s: During this time James started tackling the problem of evil-evil in the sense of strong characters and their relationship to innocent victims. It was during this period, because James was constantly experimenting in the desire to develop his technique, that the reputation of James as a difficult writer arose. His longer, more complicated sentences became his standard type of writing in this period. The important works are "The Pupil," 1891; *What Maisie Knew*, 1897; and *The Turn of the Screw*, 1898.

5. 1900s: F. O. Matthiessen, a critic, gave this first decade of the twentieth century the name "The Major Phase," and the title is apt. James in this period, with an enormous burst of energy, wrote three major novels: *The Ambassadors*, 1903, but completed in 1901; *The Wings of the Dove*, 1902; and *The Golden Bowl*, 1904. These are James's maturest efforts; they are complex, massive, and difficult novels, but they are among the best in our language. It was during this period that James began editing his own novels and writing his "Prefaces," which are essays on the problems in writing his works and studies of the novel as art, for the New York Edition of his works.

6. Final Phase: James left two unfinished works at his death: *The Sense of the Past*, 1917; *The Ivory Tower*, 1917.

MAJOR THEMES IN JAMES'S FICTION

Like all writers, James is concerned with the human situation; he is interpreting characters and life. When one refers to the major **themes** of a particular writer, he is thinking of those subjects and preoccupations that persist in a writer, that appear in many, if not most, of his works. The critic R. P. Blackmur, in *The Literary History of the United States*, distinguishes three **themes** in James's fiction: "international theme," the **theme** of the artist in conflict with society, and "the theme of the pilgrim in search of society." One can see that society is basic to James's works; he is constantly evaluating what one society maintains as its values and how these values affect groups and individuals. Many times he contrasts that particular society with the activities and mores of another society. Basically, the two societies that persist in his works are those of America and Europe.

Two dominant images emerge, therefore, in the fiction:

THE INNOCENT

James usually poses an innocent figure. The person is not stupid, not unintelligent. What James means in an innocent person is one who has not been touched by deep experience in worldly matters. These innocents are eager for life and they usually see life in others as an object for their own desires. Usually, in a James novel, these intelligent and eager creatures are corrupted and spoiled by the sophisticated ones in whom the innocents think that the virtues they would like reside. The innocents are candid, and human. They have strength and respond with deep conviction when they see their ideals corrupted. They are almost always intelligent, and they naturally, without affectation, understand good and evil, right and wrong. The sophisticated ones prey on these innocents, because they substitute experience in the world for natural decency. However, the successes of the experienced are hollow. The strong figures in James are the natural good ones.

THE INTERNATIONAL THEME

Most of the things said about the heroes and heroines of a Jamesian work apply to this basic **theme** that James mastered and matured. The international subject is the study of the American abroad. These Americans are unaware of the **conventions** and formalities of Europe; they make mistakes, they have deficiencies in tact and polish, but they have freedom, innocence, and grace, and these more than make up for their lack of experience. James contrasts the two societies very carefully: the American is not yet matured and he is awkward because he does not know how the society he is in expresses itself. He knows that there are deeper and lasting values in the society of Europe, but his natural way is usually in conflict with these values. Europe, on the other hand, does not have the vitality and youthfulness of the American world. Europe is a matter of **convention**, that is, formal responses in social situations. Every move, every act, is deliberate and committed in an established way. In James's last works, Europe does seem to represent an ideal, but the innocent, vital American remains a serious threat to the established order.

If one will examine in the following pages Henry James's *Daisy Miller*, he will see one of James's earliest examinations of the international **theme**. It is surprisingly a very full look at the whole subject in its basic forms. *Daisy Miller* looks forward to *The Portrait of a Lady* and the great accomplishment in the character of Isabel Archer and also to *The Wings of the Dove* and the more complete and subtle characterization of Milly Theale. These later works are more complicated, more difficult in style, but *Daisy Miller* presents the essential ideas inherent in the international theme.

Daisy, as a character, is an innocent, but the whole problem of innocence, especially in contrast to the influence of evil, comes out most vividly in *The Turn of the Screw*. There the entire story examines the potential meanings, the ironies and ambiguities, of this basic **theme**. Together *The Turn of the Screw* and *Daisy Miller* are two of Henry James's most popular stories. They contain his essential **themes** and his essential style. They are a good place for all students of James to begin.

THE JAMESIAN NOVEL

Henry James looked upon the novel as a work of art. In the truest sense of the word art, one can say James was one of the first writers to think of the novel in this way. James did not use the novel as a social document or as a forum for his philosophy. To James, the novel is a form complete in itself. Admittedly, he is difficult to read. The following is a synopsis of what one can expect to find in his works: First, a Jamesian novel is not a vehicle for something else. The story, plot, dialogue are complete within the work itself. Second, in a James novel, there is always what James referred to as the "central consciousness," that is, a mind and person through whom the story is being presented to the reader. James is always conscious of how the reader is hearing and seeing his story. Basically, he stays away from the omniscient narrator except for occasional comments. The omniscient narrator means that the story is told from the point of view of the author. He knows all the characters and what they are thinking and doing. James usually attempts to tell the story from the point of view of a character in the work. In *The Turn of the Screw*, James tells the story from the point of view of the first person narrator. In *Daisy Miller*, the story is seen through the mind of Winterbourne. The reader can note there that the story is never seen from Daisy's point of view. The story is about how Daisy is seen by others, especially Winterbourne. The reader should understand that James's dominating technical device is point of view, the decision that the author had made on from whose eyes, ears, and mind he is going to tell the story to the reader. Third, the reader soon realizes that in James's novels there are rarely, if ever, plain ornaments. Dialogue is never just plain talk; it is always moving the plot forward. Description always establishes a scene so that one can understand the direction of the work. Scenes are always full of meaning in relation to other things in the novel. Fourth, one can summarize all the above by saying that a Jamesian novel is always organic, all things are in relation to the whole. Nothing, not character, plot, story, scene, dialogue, description-nothing is isolated. All parts are related.

JAMES'S CRITICISM ON THE NOVEL

During his writing career James wrote many reviews, essays, and articles on writers and their works, but he made an outstanding contribution to the study of the novel in two separate parts of critical writings. First, from 1907 to 1917 there was issued a collected edition of Henry James's works. Usually this edition is referred to as "The New York Edition" by James scholars. For this collection, James selected the works, chose to leave some of his less successful works out (although some of these, such as

The Bostonians, are considered highly now), revised passages in the works, and for each volume wrote a critical preface. These prefaces contain some of the most sophisticated discussions of the art of the novel in all literature. Usually, in each preface James tried to explain how he came upon the story, what he referred to as the "germ." Then James explained what possibilities he saw in the germ and the problems he was confronted with in developing the novel. In many cases James pointed to outstanding devices, techniques, and in many other cases James pointed out some of the mistakes he felt he had made. There are further discussions of the prefaces to *The Turn of the Screw* and *Daisy Miller*. These essays are surely among the most important documents on prose fiction, for they give an insight not only into the mind of a great writer, they also reveal the art of the novel.

Second, in September, 1884, James published in *Longman's*, a magazine, an essay known as "The Art of Fiction." It was written in reply to a lecture given by a Walter Besant, a Victorian novelist and historian. Besant's lecture, "Fiction as a Fine Art," has been forgotten except by literary scholars, but James's essay has remained one of the most important studies on the art of fiction. One must realize that James was a forerunner of the present thought that the novel can be looked upon as a serious work of art. Some of the more important aspects of the essay are as follows: 1. "The only reason for the existence of a novel is that it does attempt to represent life." He goes on to say that the "novel is history." 2. "The only obligation to which in advance we may hold a novel ... is that it be interesting." James then adds that the ways to make a novel interesting are innumerable. 3. "A novel is in its broadest definition a personal, a direct impression of life: that, to begin with, constitutes its value, which is greater or less according to the intensity of the impression." 4. James agrees that a novel cannot be written without a deep sense of reality, but the reality must come from an awareness of the extent of experience. In a famous **metaphor** James explains experience: "Experience is never limited ... ; it is an immense sensibility, a kind of huge spider-web of the finest silken threads suspended in the chamber of the consciousness, and catching every airborne particle in its tissue." 5. James refers to the novel as a "living thing." In other words, it is organic. (See under the Jamesian novel.) 6. According to James, there can be no distinction between character and incident. These are complements of each other. 7. Finally, James states one of the most quoted critical ideas in the essay: "We must grant the artist his subject, his idea, his donnée: our criticism is applied only to what he makes of it." There are many other items in both the "Art of Fiction" and the "Prefaces," but the student should be aware that most of the modern terms we use about the novel, the criticism that we apply to the novel, the serious manner in which we view the novel - these and other ideas had their most serious first statement in the criticism of Henry James.

INTRODUCTION TO THE AMERICAN

The American is one of Henry James's earliest successes, and it ranks with other outstanding works that he produced in the first full decade of his long writing career, the 1870's. James was the first novelist to examine the many potential meanings in **theme** of the "international" subject. One can say that that was his unique contribution to American literature. To James, the international subject meant the study of the American, with his special innocent nature and his open and honest character, in contrast to the European, with his established society and his life dictated by **conventions** and proprieties. *The American* is James's first full, his most complete, examination of that **theme**. The subject of the novel, therefore, is how a man, an American named Christopher Newman, aspires to marry a beautiful widow in Paris, how he is rejected solely on the basis that he is an American and therefore not a nobleman, and how he finally behaves once he has been denied his love. It is a subject for romance, and that is, in Henry James's very special treatment, exactly what *The American* is.

BRIEF SUMMARY OF THE NOVEL

In May of 1868, a gentleman was resting in one of the rooms of the famous French museum, the Louvre. The gentleman, it was apparent from his dress and appearance, was an American, and he was not very much aware of the esthetic aspects of the place he was visiting. His name was Christopher Newman, and later the reader finds that he had left America, tired of his dealings, a millionaire, now decided on learning the culture of Europe. Newman saw a young lady copying a Madonna in the room and walked over to her and asked how much her picture would cost. Newman finally bought a picture from this young lady, Mademoiselle Noémie Nioche. When the girl's father, Monsieur Nioche, arrived at the gallery, Newman convinced the man to give him French lessons for hire.

Although Newman knew that the young French girl had overcharged him for the picture, he was satisfied and returned to the room he was in before. There he met an old acquaintance, named Tom Tristram, whom he had not seen for eight or nine years. On the following day, Newman visited his friend and met his wife, Mrs. Tristram. They became friendly and Mrs. Tristram gave advice to Newman on many matters. One day, in response to a question as to what Newman now wanted to do in life, the American answered that he wanted to marry well. Mrs. Tristram then told Newman one woman who would certainly please him was a young widow, Claire de Cintré. Claire had been married to Monsieur de Cintré when she was eighteen years old. The man was an evil person, but Claire had been the subject of an arranged marriage. She was now twenty-five years old and living with her family, the Bellegardes, a family of "fabulous antiquity," said Mrs. Tristram. To Newman's friend, Claire was perfection itself.

One day, Newman saw Madame de Cintré at Mrs. Tristram's place and was introduced to her. Soon, Newman tried to visit Claire at her home, but he was told that she was not there by her elder brother, the Marquis de Bellegarde. Meanwhile, Newman began his French lessons with M. Nioche and heard from him about his daughter. It seemed that Mlle. Noémie Nioche was quite an independent young lady and caused her father much concern. Newman commissioned her to do more paintings for him at the same high prices and explained that he was being kind to her so that she could earn enough money for her marriage dowry, something her father was much concerned about.

Newman told Mrs. Tristram how he had been refused admission by the Marquis and how he was disappointed. She recommended to him that he continue on his original plan of touring Europe at that time. On his trip, Newman met a Reverend Mr. Babcock, a Unitarian minister from Dorchester, Massachusetts, and the two traveled together. Eventually, they separated and went their own ways.

Newman returned to Paris in the autumn. He found that Mrs. Tristram was just as ardent in her desire to have Newman and Claire get together. One day Newman visited once again the Bellegarde residence and this time was admitted. When he was shown in, Newman found Claire and her younger brother, Valentin, there. Valentin talked a great deal with Newman, wanted to show him the house, and asked much about Newman's way of life in America. Later, Madame de Bellegarde, the wife of the Marquis, came in during tea and was introduced to Newman.

About a week later, Valentin called on Newman. The two eventually became quite friendly. Valentin had a "moral grudge" against family discipline, and he told Newman that he wished that he could have the freedom to do as he pleased, as Newman did. Newman, of course, could not understand why he could not do as he pleased. Over the next few weeks the two men became closer friends, and Newman from time to time would tell Valentin that he would ask his friend for help when they knew each other better. One day, when they were seated together, Newman asked Valentin about his family. Valentin, rather freely, told the American about his mother, a descendent of an English nobleman, and his brother, the Marquis, who at fifty years old was the head of the family and like a father to his brother and sister. Newman then told Valentin that he wanted to marry Claire and asked for Valentin's help in pleading his cause. Valentin finally agreed, but he let Newman know that it would be a difficult matter because the American was not of the nobility.

On the very next day, with the longest speech he had ever made in his life, Newman proposed to Claire, but she exacted a promise from him that he not say more on the subject to her for six months. Then, through Valentin, Newman met the dowager Marquise de Bellegarde and Claire's older brother Urbain de Bellegarde. He told them of his desire to marry Claire. He also told them that he was rich. When Madame de Bellegarde asked him, how rich, Newman quoted her a very large sum. Shortly afterwards, Newman introduced Valentin de Bellegarde to Mlle. Nioche at the Louvre.

Three days later, Newman was invited to dinner at the Bellegardes. There Valentin told him that the family favored him and that they had had a special meeting on the whole matter of his proposal. Later the Marquis told him that the heads of the family, he and his mother, had decided to allow him to court Claire, and he gave his word that he and his mother would not interfere. He added, although Newman could not understand what he meant, that he and his mother would have to have time to adjust to the change in their way of life because Newman was not a nobleman. Later the Marquise de Bellegarde told him the very same.

Newman then spent much time visiting Claire, and one day, Mrs. Bread, the maid of the Bellegardes, told Newman that his suit was going well. Newman continued with his visit for six months, but Claire realized that he did not like her mother and brother. He met at Claire's a Lord Deepmere. At the end of the six months, Newman, much more sure of himself, once again talked of marriage with Claire. She accepted him, and indicated that she liked him, but she also made it clear that it was a more difficult matter than Newman thought. Newman heard none of that and knew that they loved each other. Claire did not tell her brother, but Newman announced to Madame de Bellegarde that Claire had accepted him. He knew that they were not pleased, but they congratulated him.

Newman wanted to give an engagement party very soon, but Madame de Bellegarde strongly insisted that they would have to give him one first. At that event, a ball, given in his honor, Newman was introduced to the acquaintances of the Bellegardes. Newman was very happy. One sour note was Valentin, for he had become involved with Noémie Nioche and found himself in love with the fortune-hunter. One evening, at the opera, Valentin and a Stanislas Kapp had words over Noémie, and the two became committed to a duel, which Newman considered barbarous.

On the next day, Newman went to visit Claire, but he was met by Mrs. Bread and was told that Claire was going away. Newman sensed that something was wrong and became very upset. He was led into a room. There he went directly to Claire and asked her what had happened. Claire announced that she could not marry him and that he would have to talk to her mother and brother. Newman was shocked and he accused Madame de Bellegarde and the Marquis of interfering, but Urbain stated that they had lived up to their promise: they had not interfered with Claire's choice, but now they had decided not to accept Newman. They had commanded Claire, he said. Madame de Bellegarde told Newman that they wanted to adjust to him, but at the ball they found that they could not because he was "too commercial." Claire indicated that she had been commanded by her mother, and she would do as her mother wished.

Later, Newman spoke of his rejection with Mrs. Tristram. Just then, he received a telegram from Valentin that he was ill. When Newman arrived in Geneva, Switzerland, where the duel had taken place, he found that Valentin was dying. The two spoke, and when Valentin found that his family had commanded Claire not to marry Newman, he became greatly agitated, and just before he died, he told Newman that there was a secret involving Urbain and his mother and the death of his father. He told Newman to use it against his family to force them to allow him to marry Claire. Valentin told Newman to see Mrs. Bread and tell her that he wanted her to give the secret to Newman. Three days after the funeral, Newman visited Claire, and she told him that she was going to enter a Carmelite convent for life. Newman begged her not to make that move, but Claire indicated that she had made her resolve.

Newman went to the Bellegardes in order to make a last plea. Finding them unchanged, he told them that he knew that they had a secret and that he would find it and use it against them if they did not release Claire. The Marquis refused. Newman met Mrs. Bread in a churchyard that night. Mrs. Bread, who had been a servant to the Bellegardes for forty years, told Newman that Madame de Bellegarde had killed her husband because he did not like the match between Claire and Monsieur de Cintré. Mrs. Bread had a note in the husband's hand indicating that Madame de Bellegarde was murdering him. She gave the note to Newman. Mrs. Bread then left the employ of her mistress and came to work for Newman.

Newman finally did confront Madame de Bellegarde with the document and told her and her son that he intended to show it to their friends, beginning with a duchess he had met at the ball. The next day Urbain came to Newman. Urbain knew that he could not buy the document from Newman and told Newman that he had the opportunity to act the part of a gentleman and forget the whole thing. Newman said he wanted Claire, but the Marquis refused to entertain that. Newman did go with the note to the duchess, but he found that he could not reveal the secrets of the Bellegardes.

On the advice of Mrs. Tristram, Newman went to London for a change of scene, but he could not forget his recent experience, so he returned to New York. On receiving word that Claire had taken the veil of a nun, Newman returned to Paris. He walked the streets, came to the walls of the convent, looked at them, and decided to return to America for good. That evening, before Mrs. Tristram, he burned the note he had thought would free Claire. But Newman received one last lesson: Mrs. Tristram told Newman that it was not that the Bellegardes did not fear the note Newman had, but that they had realized that Newman was too good a man to use it against them. "It was your remarkable good nature. You see they were right," she said. Newman turned and saw that the paper was now ashes.

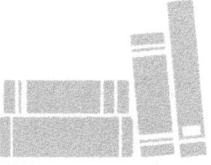

THE AMERICAN

TEXTUAL ANALYSIS

CHAPTER 1 - 5

CHAPTER ONE

"On a brilliant day in May, in the year 1868," Christopher Newman sat down to rest on a divan in a room at the Museum of the Louvre. He was staring at a Madonna by Murillo. Although he was a man unaccustomed to fatigue because he had the sort of vigor known as "toughness," Newman on this warm day had been looking at the paintings that the guide books emphasized and had been looking also at the young ladies who sat before the famous works and painted reproductions. Now he was tired with an "aesthetic headache."

Someone looking at this man would recognize that he was a "powerful specimen of an American." He was also a fine man physically. He was temperate and he did not smoke. Much more than his appearance, it was his expression, especially his eyes, that made him look so American. These eyes seemed to blend both innocence and experience, but evidently he was a practical man. For, even though he was resting, almost listlessly, and was baffled by artistic questions, he was still aware of a young lady, with a boyish coiffure, who was copying a Madonna.

The young lady went through the standard motions of the artist. She stood up and contemplated her copy and acted as though it were a necessary part of her painting. Concurrently, however, she cast sidelong glances at the man admiring her. Eventually, Newman rose, put on his hat, approached the young lady, and addressed her with the best French word he knew, "Combien?" ("how much?"). The artist was a little surprised, but the man wanted the picture. Since the girl could not speak English, she wrote on the flyleaf of the man's guidebook, "2,000 francs." He knew that that was too much money for a copy, but the girl insisted that her work was worth it when she had finished.

Then the young lady took the man's card and read his name, "Christopher Newman." She commented that American names struck her as funny. Her card, inscribed in pencil with flourishes, showed her name as "Mlle. Noémie Nioche." To him, French names were droll.

Then Noémie's father arrived, and she informed him that the American had purchased the painting from her. In French, she led her father into asking Newman if he wanted instructions in French conversation. Newman claimed that the language was difficult, but the girl quite boldly convinced her father to persist. Eventually, because he was pleased by the prospect of something he had not considered possible, Newman agreed to talk over the arrangement when M. Nioche delivered the painting of the Madonna to him.

BRIGHT NOTES STUDY GUIDE

Comment:

There are important plot matters that are quickly established in this introductory chapter, but more important are the matters of character that Henry James has put before the reader. One must remember the title of the novel, *The American*. In itself it is almost audacious to have such a title, but Henry James was very much concerned with examining a national type, as the first chapter shows, and the title is most appropriate. Christopher Newman can be recognized by the observant viewer as an American by the way he is dressed and more clearly by the expression in his eyes as he sits on the divan in the famous French museum. James emphasizes in his description that Newman is a fine specimen of a man and a practical man. He is baffled by esthetic matters and he is obviously not at home among the great paintings he has been looking at with the help of a guidebook.

These aspects of the American are very important because James in the novel will be examining how an American behaves, how he makes his choices, and how he acts in relation to a much older and more sophisticated society, the established French nobility. That is the subject of the novel, and the reader should be prepared to note carefully the many, many ways in which James refers to the topic, discusses it, and draws conclusions. It bears repeating: the extensive description of Newman as an American in the first two paragraphs of the novel is most important in that it will lead directly into the important "international subject," that is, the American in Europe theme.

The introduction of Mademoiselle Noémie Nioche is more a matter of the plot in the novel, but

it is distinctly a part of the sub-plot. Mademoiselle Nioche is a fortune hunter, an adventuress, as Newman will call her soon, and she will bring about some of the more direct actions in the novel.

A final point that the reader should recognize here (and it is something to look for in all of James's novel) is the use of Christopher Newman as what James called his "center." Newman is the one who will be experiencing the novel. He is always before the reader, and all information will come to the reader as it comes to him. Of course, in his later novels James would handle this much more sophisticatedly, but in *The American* the reader should recognize that the novel deals with Newman.

CHAPTER TWO

Newman went back to the divan where he had been sitting before. Already, only twenty minutes after he had purchased his first painting, he was thinking of becoming a collector. He realized that he had paid too much, but he decided to purchase from a young man a copy at the proper price. Newman's attention went at this moment to a man who had just entered the room. As the man stood opposite him, Newman went up to him. At first, the man did not recognize Newman, but then quickly he did. The man proved to be a Mr. Tristram. He and Newman had met last in St. Louis eight or nine years ago.

Tristram found that Newman had been in Europe seventeen days. Newman admitted that he had made his fortune. Tristram mentioned that he had lived in Paris for six years, but when he heard that Newman had just purchased a painting, he admitted that it was his wife who knew about such things. Newman remarked that he envied Tristram's being married and having children and indicated that he personally was tired of being his own master at thirty-six years of age.

Newman was then quite surprised that Tristram had not been to the Louvre before. As a matter of fact, Tristram quite directly said that he did not consider the Louvre Paris at all: "Hang it, I don't care for pictures; I prefer the reality!" Tristram then led Newman out of the museum to the Palais Royal, a cafe filled with people.

Then Tristram asked Newman to give an account of himself and his reasons for being in Europe. Tristram did not approve of the expensive hotel where Newman was staying. He suddenly questioned Newman: "You have made a pile of money, eh?" Newman replied that he had made enough. "Enough to rest awhile...to look about me, to see the world, to have a good time, to improve my mind, and, if the fancy takes me, to marry a wife."

Then, on Tristram's insistence, Newman told his story: It was "an intensely Western story." Newman left the Civil War a brigadier-general. From the time he was 14 years old he had worked hard. "He had been adventurous and even reckless. He had had good and bad fortune, and when it seemed that he could not raise any money, he finally entered San Francisco. His sole aim in life had been to make money." Only this satisfied him, and by thirty-five he had succeeded.

At this point Newman admitted that he could work hard, but he did not know how to "loaf." He told Tristram, "I have come to see Europe, to get the best out of it I can. I want to see all the great things, and do what the clever people do." He said he wanted to meet Tristram's wife.

Newman then proceeded to relate an event that took place two months before. He had come to New York for a stock-market deal, because a particular businessman who had played him a "very mean trick" was involved, and Newman wanted revenge. There was sixty-thousand dollars at stake. Newman got into a hack (a horse-drawn cab), and, being tired from traveling, fell asleep. Then he said he awoke "with the most extraordinary feeling in the world - a mortal disgust for the thing I was going to do." He was disgusted with Wall Street and took great pleasure in letting the other man get the money. He in turn told the driver to head towards the country. Then as soon as he could get out of the "game" he came to Europe.

Newman had turned his business over to a friend. Now he wanted to see "people, places, art, nature, everything, including mountains, lakes, finest pictures, handsomest churches, the most celebrated men and the most beautiful women."

On that, Mr. Tristram said, "I see I shall have to introduce you to my wife!"

Comment:

Primarily, this chapter is an introductory one as was the first and as the next will be. James continues his exposition (giving the necessary facts) of Christopher Newman by giving his background. James says that the story is an "intensely Western" one, and this is perfectly in keeping with the American aspect of Newman. He is a man of the West, the frontier of America, and his habits are those that one would expect from what was still in the 1860's the pioneer man. Then Newman is made a wealthy man, one who has made his fortune by hard work and by personal triumph. He is a business-man, a respected institution in American life. (The reader will find that the European society will hold a completely different view of this profession.)

Newman's story to Tom Tristram of how he happened to give up his business interests for the time being and how he happened to come to Paris, however, moves away from the stereotype and begins the actual personal characterization of Newman as a man. The reader should not forget that Newman gave up business in disgust because he did not approve of what he was going to do to another businessman, that is, take revenge on a person. This important personal morality (although Newman is not a religious man) plays an important part at the end of the novel, when Newman, in effect, will make the very same decision about a wholly different matter.

Tom Tristram is an interesting minor character in the novel. Actually, he is quite shallow and superficial. Already the reader knows that he has no interest in the art of Paris, for he has never visited the great museum before this day when he meets Newman. He measures Paris by its famous attractions: its women and its cafes. Tom will remain consistent throughout the novel.

One final point might be noted here: the chapter begins with the statement that Newman knew he had been overcharged by the deceitful Noémie for the picture he bought. James has many little references to the business acumen of Newman, and these references are a valuable part of Newman's character.

CHAPTER THREE

On the following day Tom Tristram did indeed introduce Newman to his wife. Mrs. Tristram was not good looking; she was in fact quite plain, so she had decided early that a woman's duty was to be pleasing. Later she put emphasis on her clothing and Paris was the right place for that. She was, all told, "eminently incomplete," a woman "full of beginnings that came to nothing."

After two or three meetings Newman and Mrs. Tristram became fast friends. Newman was not at ease in the company of women, but he spent much time listening to advice from Mrs. Tristram, although he never asked for it. Newman was the most exciting thing that had happened to Mrs. Tristram for a long time. Concerned with doing something for him, she introduced him to fifty friends while her husband complained that he never had a chance to be alone with his friend. Tom was a "shamefully idle fellow" and he irritated Newman by his way of alluding to the United States. Newman, who was not overly patriotic, defended his country. Newman did not like the circumstance, but it was simply the truth that Tom and Mrs. Tristram did not get along well at all.

Mrs. Tristram spent much time asking Newman questions about himself. She was quite concerned about how much in control of himself Newman was. She did say, however, that within six months she would see him flustered. When Newman tried to explain his feelings on being in Europe, Mrs. Tristram said, "You are the great Western Barbarian, stepping forth in his innocence and might, gazing a while at this poor effete Old World, and then swooping down on it."

The next time that Newman dined with the Tristrams, after other items of conversation, Mrs. Tristram observed to Newman that he should get married. Tom tried to discourage him, but Newman agreed and said that he wanted to marry well. "My wife must be a magnificent woman," he said. Mrs. Tristram volunteered her services to find him a wife, but Newman continued to say that after all his work and success, he now deserved a special woman, "To make it perfect...there must be a beautiful woman perched on the pile, like a statue on a monument. She must be as good as she is beautiful, and as clever as she is good." Newman continued in this vein. Then Mrs. Tristram asked him if he would mind a "foreigner." Newman replied that he had no prejudices: "Besides, I rather like the idea of taking in Europe, too," he said.

Mrs. Tristram at this point mentioned a friend of hers, a widow of twenty-five years of age, Claire de Bellegarde. She explained that Claire was French by her father, English by her mother, that she had been married to a disagreeable old man, a M. de Cintré, that her family on both sides was of "fabulous antiquity." She further explained the family had but a small fortune and lived together for economy's sake. Mrs. Tristram said that Claire was not a beauty, but beautiful.

Some days later, Newman came to the Tristram's apartment. He found a visitor there and was introduced to her: Madame Claire de Cintré. Claire was there to apologize to Mrs. Tristram that she would not be able to attend a party of hers. When she left, she invited Newman to call on her, and Mrs. Tristram was ecstatic.

One day soon, in late afternoon, Newman walked to the section of Paris where the Bellegardes lived. A lady porter allowed him to pass through the gate, but she did not know if Claire was at home. Newman crossed the court and saw a gentleman sitting on the steps of the porch and playing with a dog. Newman gave the gentleman his card and asked to see

Claire. The gentleman said that his sister was home. As the brother was to enter the house, another, older man appeared, and the two spoke. The older man looked at Newman's card and "gravely and urbanely" said to Newman that Madame de Cintré was not at home.

On his way out Newman asked the portress who the man with the dog was. She answered, "Monsieur le Comte." Then she said the other was the "Monsieur le Marquis." Newman in English said to himself, "Oh, then he's not the butler!"

Comment:

This very important chapter ends the introductory aspect of the novel. One can say that these first three chapters serve as introduction together, for at the end of the third chapter, Henry James has established his subject, the conflict of the novel, and perhaps at the very end of the chapter the final resolution. Let us examine all of these matters.

> **Mrs. Tristram is a typical Jamesian character, one that he would develop very fully in his later novels. In James's major novels, this same type character gets intimately involved with the entire plot, but Mrs. Tristram is an early example. She is what one can call a "confidante." She is the one who introduces Newman to Claire in the novel and brings about the important incident in Newman's life. She is constantly advising Newman, and she is one who knows more than the main character, because with his involvement he is not aware of all the potential answers, or problems, in his personal life. When Newman is puzzled, when he needs to know what his next step should be, and**

in the end when he needs to find out what really has happened in his Parisian affair, he will return to Mrs. Tristram. The reader should watch her in the novel.

The introductory aspect of the novel nears completion when the reader finds that Newman wants very much to marry. His ideas of what a wife should be for him are certainly not orthodox. She must be the culmination of the success he has achieved in the business world. She must be a "magnificent woman," he says. She must be "like a statue on a monument," he says. Newman is looking for an ideal woman. During much of the novel, naturally, he will idealize Claire de Cintré, and the young widow will have difficulty in living up to what he demands. A careful reader can note another interesting little allusion that has already appeared in the novel and now takes on a certain metaphoric significance. When Newman first appears in the novel, he is resting on a divan in the Louvre. However, the picture he is gazing at is a picture of the Virgin Mary, the supreme example of the ideal woman.

Newman, one can say, worships women; from all his comments, that is obvious. Whether that is another aspect of the American portrait is debatable. At any rate, the reader should note the careful preparation of Claire and Newman's immediate response that he wants to marry her.

More subtly than one at first realizes, James ends his introductory matters at the end of this chapter. Newman has tried to visit Claire. The young count he meets is Valentin de Bellegarde, who will champion his cause and become his friend in the novel. Newman is denied

THE AMERICAN

entrance into the home of Bellegarde by the Marquis, Urbain de Bellegarde. In a typical touch of humor (and there is much humor in the novel), a humor that borders somewhere between innocence and ignorance, when Newman finds that the older man, who does not want him to enter, is the Marquis, he says, "Oh, then he's not the butler." Of course, later in the novel, Newman will remain ignorant of the meaning of the French way of life and its conventions, and this same man will deny him the woman he loves. It is clear that James has completed his introduction and it is also possible that the final resolution of the novel is also clear.

CHAPTER FOUR

Early one morning M. Nioche delivered the painting of his daughter to Newman, who had forgotten about his purchase. The painting was in a large, elaborate frame, but Newman willingly paid the extra money for it. M. Nioche already had prepared a receipt for 3,000 francs instead of the original price. After their transaction, Newman asked the man about his daughter. M. Nioche was concerned that Noémie, although she was beautiful, could not marry because he could afford no dowry for her. Newman asked him what a respectable dowry would be and then suggested that Mlle. Nioche paint for him six more reproductions for which he would pay the same price he had for the first. M. Nioche was overwhelmed and grateful and offered to give Newman his lessons in French for free. Newman had forgotten about this too, but he agreed.

Every day for the following three weeks, the respectable figure of M. Nioche made its appearance before Christopher Newman and for better or for worse the French lessons continued.

Newman wanted to know about the natives and took especially an interest in the man before him and his daughter. M. Nioche emphasized his financial difficulties and the difficulties he had had with his wife, now deceased. Noémie, his daughter, was not much help financially and was somewhat of a spendthrift. She had pursued her painting after her father could no longer afford it. Frankly, the father worried about her and he said, solemnly, that he would shoot her if she were to go wrong. Already she disobeyed his wishes.

Later, M Nioche came with the message that his daughter was delighted with Newman's commission. Then the man asked the American "to respect the innocence of Mademoiselle Nioche." Newman burst out in laughter at that. When he did meet with Noémie at the Louvre to choose the paintings he wanted done for him, he asked her about herself and her father. As Newman looked at her, he thought that the father should not worry about her, for she "might do something very audacious, but she would never do anything foolish." Their choosing of paintings continued. Newman told the young lady that he would be leaving Paris soon and travelling to Switzerland.

Noémie then, quite suddenly, asked Newman why he had chosen her painting because she knew that she did not know how to paint. She said, "it irritates me to see a clever man blunder so," and told him that his commission was near impossible to complete, Newman, puzzled at her motives, told her to just do as she could, but he finally confessed that he really wanted to provide money for her dowry. Noémie had already heard this from her father, and she was disdainful of the kind of man M. Nioche wanted her to marry. Newman admitted that he knew nothing about her painting ability, but he considered her clever and left her.

Comment:

The character of the young fortune-hunter and her father's ineffective relationship with her come out in this chapter. Noémie Nioche will later in the novel aspire to higher rank and money. Already her desires are clear. It is when the sub-plot of her intrigues involves Valentin de Bellegarde, as the reader will shortly see, that the depth of her poor character will be revealed. Of course, she thinks that the American is innocent and stupid, but he already sees through her.

Monsieur Nioche is completely ineffectual as a father. He claims that if there is any violation of his daughter's innocence, he will kill her. Instead, as the novel progresses, he succumbs to her money and accepts his position as parasite on his daughter.

CHAPTER FIVE

Mrs. Tristram encouraged Newman to carry out his plan to see Europe during the summer and to return to Paris in the autumn. She assured him that Madame de Cintré was not the type to marry from one day to another. So Newman left Paris and at his own pace traveled through Belgium, Holland, The Rhineland, Switzerland, and Northern Italy. He was a good tourist, made his own decisions on excursions, but tried to see everything.

By chance, Newman formed a traveler's partnership with a Reverend Benjamin Babcock, a young Unitarian minister from Dorchester, Massachusetts. The two were quite different in character, and in the evenings Babcock would retire early to think over whether he should be traveling with someone like Newman, who the minister felt suffered from "moral reaction" (he was not religious, that is). Babcock distrusted the European life and temperament. The minister did try on some evenings to infuse some "spiritual starch" into the epicurean attitudes of Newman, but he was not successful.

The two traveled together to Venice, but then one night Babcock announced that they had to part company because he was constantly irritated by the extravagant way that Newman looked at things. Newman accepted his decision. A few days later, the American received a letter from his departed companion. The letter explained that the young minister was perplexed by Newman's caring only for the pleasure of the hour, by his "reckless confidence in pleasure," by his not realizing that art and life were very serious matters.

Newman had pause to think about the letter, but instead of writing an answer he purchased a small ivory statuette of a monk kneeling and praying, but under the folds of his gown one could see a chicken hung around his waist, and sent it to Babcock. Newman's motives in sending this valuable little piece were not clear.

The American continued his travels. During the autumn he reflected on the trip and realized that he did not regret his decision to come to Europe. But now he did not know the next step. It was four months ago, but he still remembered the eyes of the beautiful woman he had met in Mrs. Tristram's apartment. He wondered if the next step in his life would be with that woman.

Then Newman, who was not accustomed to writing letters, sent off a friendly long note to Mrs. Tristram. Newman explained that he had seen much and wanted to see more, perhaps Damascus and Baghdad. He said he would return directly to Paris if he had word that Claire would be home to him if he called. Then Newman explained that he had traveled with a Unitarian minister who broke off his companionship because he considered the American "low-minded, immoral, a devotee of 'art for art'!" Following that, he continued, he traveled with an Englishman, but that man left because he found the American too virtuous and too stern a moralist.

Comment:

This chapter of Newman's travels in Europe seems at first glance an interlude before the important matter of Newman's involvement with Madame de Cintré, but it is much more than that. Up to this time, the novel has presented Newman basically as a type. He is through and through an American, perhaps even The American. It is very easy to read the novel in that way, but Henry James was too good a novelist, too careful a craftsman, to allow his character to be so rigidly stylized. Although there has been some careful characterization before, it is in this chapter that James, through contrast, develops even more the person of Christopher Newman.

> **First, Newman is put into direct contrast to the young Reverend Babcock. The Unitarian minister is disturbed and puzzled by the free nature of Newman. He is intolerant of Newman's desires for pleasure and his lack of a moralistic point of view as he looks at the art he is seeing. The Reverend Babcock is the rigid, moral, narrow, suspicious, and limited American, surely a type quite different from the one James is presenting in the novel.**
>
> **There is a second, not so obvious, contrast in the chapter. In his letter to Mrs. Tristram, Newman**

alludes briefly to the Englishman who found Newman too virtuous and too stern a moralist. It is with this brief stroke that James accomplishes most. Newman falls somewhere between the unthinking morality of the rigid American type and the truly European understanding of life and society. The point, however, is more significant than the previous statement would indicate. The reader must be aware that he is reading of a type, but he is also reading of a personal drama.

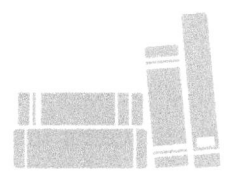

THE AMERICAN

TEXTUAL ANALYSIS

CHAPTERS 6 - 10

CHAPTER SIX

Newman returned to Paris before the summer was over and settled in some rooms selected for him by Tom Tristram. Mrs. Tristram, as usual, did not agree with anything her husband chose, but Newman, who professed to know nothing about the furnishings of lodgings, settled in the rooms on the Boulevard Haussmann, rooms that were lavishly decorated.

One day, Mrs. Tristram told Newman that Claire de Cintré had returned from the country, and of course Newman was interested. Mrs. Tristram told him that when she saw Claire, the beautiful lady was crying because she was suffering. On Newman's insistence, Mrs. Tristram explained that Claire was suffering at the hands of her wicked mother and "her Grand Turk of a brother." Newman commented that the lady should not allow that, but he was informed that it was the custom that a daughter obey the head of the family. That family, Mrs. Tristram told Newman, was planning to marry off Claire a second time, and the girl was objecting. Newman insisted that in America a girl is never subjected to such compulsion. Mrs. Tristram then told the American that he should swoop down like an eagle and free the girl by marrying her. The persistent Mrs. Tristram reported of seeing Claire a second time, and although there were no tears that time, Claire was "cold, calm, and hopeless."

A few days later, in the early evening, Newman went to the home of the Bellegardes on the Rue de l'Université. He was announced and ushered in this time, and in a large room he recognized by the firelight Claire and another gentleman, whom Claire motioned to as her brother. The gentleman greeted Newman cordially. Newman had mixed feelings about being in the house, but the original impression that Claire had made on him at first seemed even stronger now.

Their conversation began with references to Mrs. Tristram and Newman's native country. Then Newman asked the other two if they did not find their house isolated. Claire answered that their entire family had been born there and they liked it. When Newman asked them how old the house was, Valentin, Claire's brother, looked up at an elaborately engraved piece of marble above the fireplace and read the date 1627. Newman commented on the architecture of the house, which caused Valentin to ask him if he were interested in architecture in general. Newman answered that during the summer he seen some four hundred and seventy churches.

Then, just when Newman was thinking the younger brother to be impudent, Valentin offered to show Newman the house. Madame de Cintré was visibly surprised by the offer, but before the two could begin, Claire asked Valentin to ring for tea. Right after the servant brought the tray, a young and pretty lady hurried into the room and began to speak rapidly in French. Claire introduced her as her sister-in-law, the Marquise. The conversation became somewhat awkward at the moment, but Newman was intent on observing the beautiful Claire, who struck him as being not proud at all in the way Mrs. Tristram had described.

Eventually, the Marquise de Bellegarde asked Newman about his business in America. Newman answered that he at one time sold leather and later manufactured bathtubs. He had been successful with the former and had lost money with the latter. After some further conversation, Newman said that he would like to visit again and he hoped that Madame de Cintré would be in. Claire asked her brother to invite Newman again, but Valentin asked Newman if he were a brave man. Finally, the Marquise, impatient with the other two, told Newman to call on her.

Comment:

In the novel, whenever Newman is introduced to people, the great concern of the moment will be the American aspect of Newman. The contrast between Newman and the people will be persistently examined. Even Claire wonders about the American background of Newman. It is perhaps obvious that the Europeans would think that the manufacture of bathtubs is typical of Americans.

The other aspect of the international subject begins quietly in this chapter. When Newman asks Claire and her brother about the age of the house and hears "1627," he does not as yet realize the important dimension of age and venerability. Of course, the fact that Newman does not care about the age of the

house is part of the fabric of his character and mind. Newman is accustomed to doing things directly, without waste, just as he is willing to go directly to the house of the Bellegardes without wasting time.

CHAPTER SEVEN

About a week later, very late in the evening, the young Count de Bellegarde, Valentin, called on Newman. Still thinking him somewhat impudent, Newman greeted him rather coldly and told him to remain if that was his desire. Newman sensed that there was something he liked about the young man, but Valentin struck him as being, even with his excellent English, a "foreigner to his finger-tips." Valentin informed Newman that his sister had asked him to make the visit in order to apologize for acting like a "lunatic" during Newman's visit to them.

Valentin then asked Newman about his stay in France and whether he was enjoying himself or not. He offered to help him enjoy Paris, but then said that it was foolish for him, who was a failure in life, to help Newman, who was apparently so successful. This conversation served as an introduction to the night the two men spent together, for they talked until they heard the morning hours striking from a far-off belfry. Valentin was a young man who was destined to play the part of a gentleman of a noble family. He had had the proper schooling, but he had never lost his personal spontaneity. "He had been tied with so short a rope in his youth that he had now a mortal grudge against family discipline."

Valentin expressed envy of Newman's liberty and explained that he had no profession, nor knew how to work, because he was a Bellegarde. Of course, Newman was not able to understand all this, especially with his American attitude that a man worked as he pleased. At any rate, Valentin said that he hoped he could help Newman someday, at which Newman replied that something might come up someday later.

During the next three weeks, Valentin and Newman became close friends. Though they were quite different from each other, each seemed to amuse the other. Newman was quite surprised by Valentin's apartment, which contained oddities collected by the owner, all placed in picturesque disorder throughout. Bellegarde, himself, amused Newman by his talk about his private life. He liked especially to have something to say about women in his life.

On the other hand, the loquacious Valentin was greatly interested in Newman's experiences. Valentin wanted to know why a man with Newman's background would remain in Paris. Newman avowed that there was something, but told his friend that he would find out later.

That particular something very much in Newman's mind was Madame de Cintré, whom Newman had seen twice more, but each time there were many men and women callers at her place. Newman did not say anything to Valentin because he was circumspect and enjoyed keeping this whole thing to himself. One day, however, Valentin took Newman to the apartment of a Madame Dandelard, a little Italian lady who had married a Frenchman and who now sat and told of the beatings that she suffered from her husband once he had squandered his fortune. Newman wondered why Valentin did not send his sister to advise the young lady, but the Count demurred by saying that his sister was not the type to be involved with such a woman.

On that one evening, Newman asked Valentin to come to his apartment, and Valentin, always looking forward to an evening of conversation, quickly assented.

Comment:

Much more carefully and slowly, Henry James will now begin his full introduction of the European society and its characters that will play such a significant part in the life of Newman. It is fitting, and indicative of the way the novel must be understood, that James begins examining his aristocrats by making Valentin de Bellegarde a friend of the American. Valentin shows that the European aristocracy have come to their end so far as they are related to the world outside of their circle of friends and acquaintances. Valentin has no profession, he is incapable of holding any specific job. Newman, the American, cannot understand why he does not go out and do something in life without worrying about the family decisions. Valentin, however, belongs to an aristocratic family, and he must live according to its rules. The personal spontaneity that he has, has bothered the society he belongs to and Valentin holds a moral grudge against family discipline. It is that family discipline that is so significant in the novel.

In summary form, we can say that James begins unfolding the position of the aristocracy by showing that their lives are in decay. Their house is dark and isolated. Their younger son is trying to break away. The sense that one has is the sense of decay. With a single touch in a character who will not reappear in the novel, Madame Dandelard, James punctuates firmly the seeming death sentence that had been pronounced sometime ago.

CHAPTER EIGHT

When they sat down in Newman's apartment, the American started with, "Tell me something about your sister." It was the first time that Newman had asked Valentin anything concerning Madame de Cintré. Valentin, as he put it, could not help but "rhapsodize" over his sister. He considered her, in answer to Newman's questions, kind, charitable, gentle, generous, clever, gay. When Newman asked if she was unhappy, Valentin hesitated somewhat, then admitted that his sister's life had not been exactly happy. Then Valentin explained that when Claire was eighteen, her mother and older brother had arranged a marriage for her with the sixty-year-old Monsieur de Cintré. Valentin called him an "odious old gentleman" who lived a short time after the marriage. On his death his family pounced on his money and certain facts, which revealed irregular practices, appeared and caused Claire to disclaim any right to the money. Claire's mother was so upset that she allowed Claire to drop the suit only with the promise that Claire would do exactly what she and her older brother commanded for a period of ten years.

Newman asked about the mother and brother. His brother, Valentin explained, was upwards of fifty and had been a father to him and his sister. His mother, he explained, was also remarkable, a daughter of an English nobleman, the Earl of St. Dunstan. Her family went back only to the sixteenth century, while the French background went to the ninth century, the time of Charlemagne.

After hearing all this, Newman got to his point. He asked Valentin, "Do what you can to make your sister think well of me." Then he told him that he wanted to marry Madame de Cintré.

Valentin reacted with extreme surprise. Newman tried to explain himself, but Valentin did not know whether he was pleased or horrified. Newman could not understand why he would be horrified. Valentin said, "you are not noble, for instance." Newman insisted that, although he did not have a title, he certainly was noble. He even stated that if he liked her well enough, if she suited him, that is, he would go up to a duchess and ask her to marry him. Newman felt that he could offer a woman anything she wanted, but he did have very high standards. Valentin listened to all this. The more he listened the more he saw in the proposal. He thought it was unfortunate that Newman would not be able to understand his explanations of the possible difficulties. Finally, Valentin agreed to help Newman.

Valentin warned Newman that both his mother and brother were strange and that he would have to be prepared for them. He reminded the American that they were "eight hundred years old." Newman said that that fit in exactly with his plans. At the very end of the conversation, Valentin said that one reason he was helping Newman was that he liked him, but he also said that there was another reason. Newman thought that he meant that he also disliked his brother (and would therefore oppose him by supporting Newman). When Valentin took his leave, Newman sat before his fire and stared into the blaze.

Comment:

> Valentin's explanation of his sister's marriage to the old and dishonest Monsieur de Cintré and the part that family played in the arrangement become significant in Mrs. Bread's story of the whole background of the family, especially the mother and the brother, later. (See Summary of Chapter Twenty-two.) At the present, however, the reader should keep in mind that the mother and brother extract a promise from Claire that she do what she is told by them.

> Valentin's few words about his mother and brother are a good introduction to these characters.

The brother is the head of the family, in that he is the oldest male and is so much older than his brother and sister. Valentin remarks that his mother is also a special person, but the emphasis he puts on the ages of the families involved obviously falls on deaf ears so far as Newman is concerned.

Never one to waste time, Newman then reveals that he wants to marry Claire, but he does not really pay special note to Valentin's reaction, except to claim that he is noble although he does not have a title. He will realize later how important a matter that is. Valentin is right when he decides that Newman would not understand the whole thing anyway.

Valentin's willingness to help is another matter. One is troubled to decide if he actually wants to help Newman, if he wants to crack the rigidity of the family, or if he really would like to disrupt the haughty brother.

CHAPTER NINE

Newman went to see Claire de Cintré the next day. When he was shown into the drawing-room he wondered if her brother had had an opportunity to speak to her yet. He wondered what the effect would be. Claire finally appeared, and indeed Valentin had spoken to her just an hour before. She told Newman that she was seeing him now because her brother had asked her to.

Then, with directness and firmness and without any sense of confusion, Newman said, "What I told him last evening was this: that I admired you more than any woman I had ever seen, and that

I should like immensely to make you my wife." He then stood up before the amazed woman and delivered the longest speech in his life. Newman told her among other things, "I could have said it the first time I saw you. Really, I had seen you before; I had seen you in imagination; you seemed almost an old friend.... You are just the woman I have been looking for, except that you are far more perfect." Newman then said that he knew the social circumstances, but he was sure that he would make a good husband for her.

Claire de Cintré had sat through the speech of Newman, but now she rose, looking very serious, and told her suitor that she appreciated all he had said but she had decided not to marry. Newman begged her not to say that; he begged for the opportunity to make her happy. Madame de Cintré then asked Newman to leave if he was going to discuss this matter, but Newman persisted. Finally, Claire said she would continue to see Newman if he made a solemn promise not to discuss the matter for a long time. When Newman asked how long, she replied, "For six months." Newman promised.

That evening Newman saw Valentin de Bellegarde on the Boulevard. Anxious to know if Claire had said anything to him, Newman asked him if he had seen his sister. Valentin admitted that he had, at dinner, and he wanted to know what could have happened at their meeting. Newman quickly told him that he had proposed to his sister. Valentin was quite surprised at Newman's desire not to waste time. He then told Newman that he must now introduce him to his brother. Newman was ready.

Comment:

Newman's awkward, yet eloquent "longest speech" is one of the high points in the novel. It is completely in character, and in accordance with the way that James develops the novel, that Newman would waste no time in making his proposal to the beautiful Madame de Cintré. In contrast to the way that the Europeans will behave with him, Newman is direct and honest. Of course, he is also innocent. Claire, however, knows the complications of what the proposal actually means, and one cannot criticize her for wanting a long time to find out what her own emotions are. She cannot help but be surprised; she cannot help but know that her mother and brother will react very strongly.

CHAPTER TEN

Newman continued to see the Tristrams regularly, but Mrs. Tristram was convinced not regularly enough, for she thought that Newman was now concerned with high society. Curiously enough, Mrs. Tristram was a little disappointed that her plans for Newman were working so well. For example, she tried to explain to Newman that Claire was not so outstanding as he now believed. Mrs. Tristram, however, was capable of being just on certain occasions. One such occasion occurred when Newman told her he had proposed to Madame de Cintré. Mrs. Tristram considered the whole thing a triumph. When Newman emphasized that Claire had not accepted him yet, Mrs. Tristram explained that it must be considered a triumph because Madame de Cintré had not refused to see him again after the proposal. Mrs. Tristram was at a loss at what it was in Newman that was so winning for a lady like Claire.

It was immediately after this conversation that Valentin came to Newman to conduct him to the meeting with his family on the Rue de l'Université. Valentin told Newman that he was already being discussed in the family and it seemed that the Marquise de Bellegarde had taken a particular fancy to him. A little later that evening, Valentin escorted Newman into a room of the Bellegardes' house. Newman recognized the young Marquise de Bellegarde at the piano. She stopped playing when Newman went over to the older woman sitting before the fire. Newman shook hands with her, and Madame de Bellegarde began the conversation with "I ought to have seen you before." Newman felt that she was a "formidable, inscrutable little woman." She did resemble her daughter in Newman's mind, but the mother's "white, intense, respectable countenance, with its formal gaze, and its circumscribed smile suggested a document signed and sealed; a thing of parchment, ink and ruled lines." Newman reflected, "She is a woman of **conventions** and proprieties; her world is the world of things immutably decreed."

Madame de Bellegarde asked Newman if he were an American as if she did not know how one spoke to one. The effusive Marquise came over, concerned over her evening dress. Newman looked around the room and thought it shabby. Then Valentin interposed and asked his mother if she approved of Newman, but the old woman replied that she did not have time enough to know the American.

At this point, Valentin's older brother entered. As Newman was introduced to him, the marquis claimed he was delighted, but he did not offer his hand. Newman said to himself as he looked at Marquis Urbain de Bellegarde, "He is the old woman at second-hand."

Urbain, who was prepared to go out that evening with his wife and his brother, begged to have a little conversation with Newman. He said that he had heard that Newman was in business. Newman said that that was over and that he was now "loafing" in Paris. Then Urbain asked Newman if he was interested in anything in particular. Newman replied that he was interested in manufacturing, but added, "I can't say I have had any specialty. My specialty has been to make the largest possible fortune in the shortest possible time." Then Newman explained to the Marquis that he had been working from the time he was a mere boy and that he had stopped going to school when he was ten. One of his sisters (he had two) was married, he said, to the owner of the largest India-rubber house in the West. Newman turned to Madame de Bellegarde and said to her, although he found it somewhat disagreeable to do so, that he was not absolutely idle: "I will tell you my project; perhaps you can help me. I want to take a wife." Madame de Bellegarde claimed that she was not a matchmaker, but Newman said he thought she was.

At this point, Valentin reappeared in the room and announced that Claire had decided to accompany her family on their night out. Madame de Bellegarde was surprised, as was the Marquis, because Claire had not been out socially for three years. Madame de Bellegarde was surprised that her daughter had not asked her. The Marquis was puzzled at why she should have chosen this particular affair to attend. Claire finally entered, dressed in a white gown, and caused Newman to think that she looked "tremendously handsome."

After the others had left, Newman commented to Madame de Bellegarde that he considered her daughter beautiful. The mother cautioned him that she was strange. Newman then expressed the hope that "she will consent, some day, to marry me." Madame de Bellegarde rose from her place and indicated that she did not favor Newman's "project." Newman asked her only to suffer it. The old woman then called herself proud and meddlesome. Newman replied that he was very rich. When Madame de Bellegarde asked him, how rich, he replied with a very large, round number. The old woman knew he was frank, and Newman excused himself for the evening.

> Comment:

With this chapter, Henry James has presented Christopher Newman's formidable adversary, the old Madame de Bellegarde. Newman realizes that she is a strong figure. He does not underestimate her, but he does not count how completely in command of affairs she actually is. The reader must realize immediately that Madame de Bellegarde is a woman of conventions and proprieties. "Her world is the world of things immutably decreed." What Henry James is establishing here, with the age of the family, its long heritage, its stuffy and threadbare house, is the fact that Newman is trying to enter a family that has done things according to the established rules of their own society. Their decisions are made by the established mores of their way of life. Newman is an intruder into that society. He wants to change that way of life. In Madame de Bellegarde he has found a difficult, strong guardian of the past, and of tradition.

Newman's reflection that the Marquis Urbain de Bellegarde is "the old woman at second-hand" is very incisive as the reader will see later. He is aloof and stiff, always condescending in his attitude towards Newman.

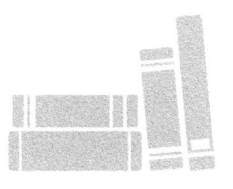

THE AMERICAN

TEXTUAL ANALYSIS

CHAPTERS 11 - 15

CHAPTER ELEVEN

Newman had not gone to see M. Nioche on his return to Paris; he was not interested in taking up his French lessons now that he had other things to do. The old man, however, found that the American had returned and came to his new rooms. Newman inquired about Mademoiselle Nioche of the father, and as usual, the old man was quite seriously concerned about her. He informed Newman that his daughter was going to the Louvre all the time, but she evidently was accomplishing nothing. She had not, he said, done anything on the commission that Newman had given her.

To fulfill a promise to the old man, Newman went to the Louvre to see Noémie. As he was making his way to the hall where the Italian masters were hung, he met Valentin de Bellegarde, who was pleased to see an acquaintance because he himself was in poor humor. Valentin said that he had no interest in the paintings that day because he was at the Louvre only to meet an English cousin who was visiting Paris for a week with her husband. He had been waiting twenty minutes and he was upset.

Valentin decided to go along with Newman on this meeting. Newman explained that he was going to meet a certain young lady. When they came to the gallery where Mademoiselle Nioche was supposed to be working, Newman saw her at her easel, but instead of painting, she was looking across the room at two well-dressed women. Newman went up to her with Valentin and introduced the Count to her. She said that she thought Newman had forgotten her, but he said that he never would. Newman told her that he had heard that she was not painting. She complained that she did not know how to paint, and she asked Valentin to judge what she had on her easel. He in turn quite frankly told her that she ought not to paint.

Mademoiselle Nioche turned the conversation to Newman's trip, but she was evidently more interested in the well-dressed ladies. She dipped her brush into a glob of red paint and drew a horizontal line across her canvas. When Newman wanted to know why, she said in effect that that was the sign of the truth about herself. Valentin was greatly interested in the young girl.

M. Nioche in his characteristic shuffle appeared and whisked his daughter away. Valentin told Newman that he considered the girl remarkable, but Newman warned him that he considered her an "adventuress" and that her father claimed he would kill her if she got into trouble. At about this point, Valentin felt a poke in the back from the parasol of his evidently angry cousin.

Comment:

It is in this chapter that James brings the sub-plot into contact with the main plot of the novel. The meeting of Valentin and Noémie is important because it will bring about the true tragedy in the novel, the death of Valentin. That tragedy, however, James will use to reveal the facts in the background of the Bellegarde family. The constant nature of Noémie's character is emphasized in the chapter in the way she keeps on eyeing the well-dressed ladies in the museum.

CHAPTER TWELVE

Three days after Newman had met the Bellegarde family, he came home to find the calling card of the Marquis. The next day he received an invitation to dinner from the Marquise. Newman broke another engagement and went to the Bellegardes. The greetings he received seemed rather stiff, although Valentin took great pains to explain that they were not. The Marquise extended her hand without looking at him, and Claire went on telling one of her nieces a fairy tale.

Eventually, dinner was announced and Newman found himself seated with the family. The conversation during dinner seemed strained to him. Urbain de Bellegarde particularly looked uncomfortable, and even Valentin seemed nervous. After dinner, the Marquis led the way into the smoking room, and Valentin, unable to keep quiet any longer, broke out with the news that the family had decided to accept Newman as a suitor. He explained that there had been a family meeting and that even he was allowed to testify. The Marquis was obviously upset with Valentin's lack of tact, but he too verified that the family was willing to accept Newman as a suitor to the Comtess de Cintré, as he referred to his sister. He took great pains to emphasize that Madame de Bellegarde would have to speak to Newman. Urbain, in a very roundabout way, tried to explain painfully that the family would have to make great adjustments to the acceptance of Newman, especially since he was not of their kind, a nobleman, and since he was a businessman. Valentin mocked his brother, and somewhat tactlessly told him that it was a good thing that Newman did not understand what he was saying. Newman, on his part, admitted that he did not understand what the Marquis was talking about, but he said that he was interested only in marrying the Marquis' sister, not the Marquis.

Newman was shown back to the drawing room so that he could have the words of old Madame de Bellegarde. In his absence several visitors had arrived. Since the others were occupied, the Marquise de Bellegarde came over to Newman and informed him that she knew his situation. She said that she wanted to ally herself with him, because both of them were new to the family. Newman said that he was not interested in joining the family but in taking Madame de Cintré out of it. Newman went to join Claire, who was speaking to an older woman. Claire introduced Newman to Madame de Rochfidele, who was greatly interested in meeting him because she had never seen an American. The old lady lifted an antique eye-glass and inspected Newman. Then Madame de Bellegarde approached with Monsieur de Rochfidele, who was not so surprised by the American because he had met as a youngster "the great Dr. Franklin."

Finally, the guests were shown out, and Madame de Bellegarde had her opportunity to speak with Newman. She assumed that her son had informed him of their decision. She wanted to add a point; she said, "We are stretching a point; we are doing you a great favor." She made emphatic that her entire family was proud: she, her son, her daughter, and even Valentin, if the proper time were to come to him. The old woman continued, "I shall not enjoy having my daughter marry you, and I shall not pretend to enjoy it. If you don't mind that, so much the better." She vowed that they would hold to their word of not interfering with his proposal to Claire. Newman was not so sure that the old woman would not learn to like him.

Newman then spoke to Claire and told her that he would call often. Then Valentin came to the American and asked him if he enjoyed his "permit." Valentin turned the conversation to another matter. He asked Newman if he had seen his venerable old friend, M. Nioche. Newman said he had. Valentin asked if the old man looked angry, or if he was carrying a gun. Newman replied that the man looked in good spirits. Valentin then laughed and told Newman in good spirits. Valentin then laughed and told Newman that Mademoiselle Nioche had left her father's house and obviously the old man was not so grieved as he claimed he would be. Now, Valentin felt, he could see the girl at his pleasure.

Comment:

One has visions and thoughts of what the family conference was like when the Bellegardes held court to decide on whether to allow Newman to be a suitor of Claire. It is typical of James to leave out such scenes, and perhaps the reader who is new to James should understand why. One must remember that the novel has for its center the experience of Christopher Newman. All the scenes occur in his presence, and the subject of the book is his reactions and decisions to the individual scenes. James is interested in the meeting, but that is not his subject. It is the American.

Urbain de Bellegarde speaks for the family. He is insulting, but he thinks he is right in trying to tell Newman that the family would have to make adjustments to the idea of Newman's marrying Claire. Newman of course cannot understand why his being a businessman should be held against him, but Henry James is now drawing the lines much sharper. There are involved two completely opposing sets of values here. Newman is natural and innocent; the Bellegardes are formal and act according to rules that their society has prescribed.

The reader must pause for a moment and consider the promise that the mother and brother are making. Later, this will be a very important point in the novel. Urbain says that the family will not interfere with Newman's proposal to Claire and her decision. Madame de Bellegarde says this plainly.

Madame de Bellegarde is very direct in telling Newman that she cannot approve of him, that it is not her liking that Newman shall be the husband of her daughter. The reader should distinguish between her way of saying things and that of her son Urbain.

James continues to exaggerate the way that the aristocratic Europeans have difficulty in establishing in their minds exactly what an American is in the brief exchange with Madame de Rochfidele, who eyes and measures Newman with her antique glass. It is almost as though Newman were a savage from the western part of the world.

CHAPTER THIRTEEN

Over the next six weeks Newman kept to his word of visiting often at the home of the Bellegardes. Newman thought that he was not really in love, but he did feel a deep tenderness for Madame de Cintré. The more he saw her the more she pleased him, and one could venture to say that Newman did not understand that the scientist would call what he was experiencing love. Newman did not make love to Claire, and he did not make any sentimental speeches. Many times he would visit and sit quietly in the drawing-room. He did tell her hundreds of stories about America, and he noticed that she had a natural gaiety. Still he felt that she harbored a deep tearful secret.

On many evenings, in deference to Claire, he would sit next to Madame de Bellegarde. He would ask the old lady if she would be able to tolerate him that particular evening when he greeted her. To Mrs. Tristram Newman observed that he felt that the old lady might be an old sinner. "I shouldn't wonder if she had murdered someone - all from a sense of duty," he said. Newman thought that a favorable comment. On the other hand, he had no favorable thoughts about the Marquis, who always seemed rigidly on guard in Newman's presence. Newman, on his part, was becoming more and more relaxed.

One afternoon, when Newman called, he was asked to wait by a servant he had seen before, but had never spoken with. The servant, Mrs. Bread, an Englishwoman, lingered about the room and began to speak to Newman. Mrs. Bread had come from England with Madame de Bellegarde and had been with the family for forty years. She said she was greatly interested in the family but especially in Madame de Cintré. She said she approved of Newman and hoped he would marry Claire and take her away, the farther the better. When Newman suggested that she accompany him and Claire after they had married, Mrs. Bread very readily agreed.

Claire arrived and Mrs. Bread left through another door. Although Newman and Claire were careful never to discuss her family, she turned the conversation to her younger brother and told Newman that she did not like the way he spoke of him. Newman did not realize he was being disrespectful, but he said that he would watch over the Count for his sister.

At the end of one quiet evening, as Newman was leaving, Claire came to Newman and said, "You do not like my mother and brother." Newman answered, "No." The next time they saw each other, they returned to the same conversation. Newman felt that the disliking of him by Claire's family was more important than his own feelings. Claire later told Newman that her brother and mother, although they did not like him, had not spoken ill of him. Newman was sincere in saying to Claire that he considered that quite decent of them.

On the evening of that conversation, Urbain de Bellegarde and his mother, both in the best spirits that Newman had ever seen them in, escorted into the room a man that Madame de Bellegarde introduced as Lord Deepmere, their cousin. Lord Deepmere was thirty-three years old, with a bald head, a short nose, and no front teeth in the upper jaw. He was shy and laughed a great deal. The Marquis informed Newman that Lord Deepmere was English, a man with immense property.

Before he left that evening, Newman thanked the Marquis for sticking to his bargain so well.

Comment:

Two innocent meetings in this chapter have a deep influence on Newman and the rest of the novel, but Newman does not at all recognize the further possibilities at this point. Newman is assuming at this point, and he has every reason to, that his suit is going well according to the best hopes he has.

> The first meeting in the chapter is with Mrs. Bread, the long-time servant of the Bellegardes. Many critics have noted that Mrs. Bread has a mechanical function in the novel, that at a given point she is brought into the novel only because she will reveal to Newman the dark secret of the Bellegarde family. To a very great extent, every reader should recognize that that is true. There are, however, some interesting character traits that come out in her, and she does have more life than many are willing to admit. At this point, suffice it to say, the reader should note Mrs. Bread because she will be important later.
>
> Lord Deepmere too is introduced late, but he too will play his role in the novel. One should note the glee and happiness, so very, very uncharacteristic, with which the Bellegardes, Madame and Urbain, introduce the nobleman with immense property. This is the first hint that Madame de Bellegarde has definite plans for him.

CHAPTER FOURTEEN

The next time Newman visited Claire he had something quite definite on his mind. The six months were over, he informed

Claire, and he intended to take up where he had left off. Claire revealed that she had thought about it a great deal, and she was willing to marry him. She did add, however, that she felt some fear, which Newman tried to dispel. She felt that things would not be so simple as Newman thought. Too elated to think otherwise, Newman decided that the only reason Claire was willing to marry him, especially with the difficulty of her family's understanding her decision, was her love for him.

Newman came back the next day and met Mrs. Bread in the vestibule. She said she knew that Claire had accepted him although no one had told her, and she cautioned Newman to get the marriage over quickly. Mrs. Bread showed Newman into the living room. Claire quickly came to him and told him that she had not told her mother yet. The old lady overheard these comments, and asked her daughter if she had consented. Claire told her she had. Immediately, Madame de Bellegarde called for Urbain. The young Marquise congratulated Newman. Then Urbain and Valentin appeared and they too were apprised of Claire's decision. Newman could hardly suppress his feelings.

Newman and Claire realized that both the Marquis and Madame de Bellegarde did not approve. Claire told Newman that she minded terribly, even when he tried to insist that she pay no attention. Madame de Bellegarde showed surprise that Newman had already telegraphed back to America that he was to be married.

Newman came back with answers to his telegrams. Obviously, Madame de Bellegarde did not enjoy them at all, but Claire laughed immoderately at some of the humorous comments from Newman's friends in them. Very shortly afterwards, Newman informed Madame de Bellegarde that he intended to hold a party and invited the old woman. Without warning, Madame de

Bellegarde said that things should be done in order, and since he wanted it, she invited Newman to a fête on the 25th of the month. This struck Newman as a handsome proposal and he was quite willing to put his off.

Valentin escorted Newman away from the house that night, and he tried to explain that the party was something that had come to his mother in an instant, that she was driven to the wall and was forced into it. Newman could not understand why it should be so, but Valentin assured him that the whole thing would be done handsomely.

Comment:

One of the major criticisms of the novel that has persisted through the years is the fact that Claire is not completely drawn. It is true that James saw fit to draw her mother and brother much more completely, but there are given many little insights into her character that a reader should not ignore. In the first place, a reader must understand that Claire's accepting of Newman is a total and daring decision for the young window. She knows, as Newman does not, the full implication of her willingness to marry outside the world of nobility and family selection. In a time when we measure love by its grossest manifestations, its outward appearances, it is hard to accept the fact that Claire's love is deep and abiding. In no other way, however, can one interpret her emotions. One must know that she is in love with the new man in the novel. She is willing to give up everything that she has been taught, everything that represents the world as she knows it, for him. Love cannot be measured more highly than that. Perhaps, she sees her marriage as a way to free herself of her family. There is no question, as one finds later, that that thought runs through her mind. But she is a happy girl. She is feeling freedom, as her immoderate laughing at the facetious telegrams definitely indicates.

> Madame de Bellegarde's sudden and un-planned-for decision to give a party at which the family will introduce Newman is an important part of the world of the Bellegardes. The family is of very small fortune, it has seen its better days, but appearances must be maintained, and Madame de Bellegarde is not about to allow Newman to outdo her and break tradition by giving his party first. That the decision is laden with dangerous possibilities Newman cannot conceive as yet.

CHAPTER FIFTEEN

The things that Valentin had told Newman about Noémie and M. Nioche explained partially why Newman had not seen the old man lately. Valentin filled in some more details on the recent life of the attractive girl. Since a month had elapsed from his last seeing M. Nioche, Newman was concerned that the old man might have committed suicide, so he decided to visit him. When he called at the apartment, the man was not there, but a glove-cleaner told him that he could be found at the Café de la Patrie. Newman walked the short distance and saw M. Nioche sipping a drink at a table with a woman. The well-dressed woman proved to be Mademoiselle Nioche, who was visiting her father.

Newman told the girl that he did not expect to find her with her father because he had heard that she was living someplace else. She knew that he had gotten his information from Valentin. Newman, quite directly, told Noémie that he was disappointed in her, that she could have remained an honest woman. The girl had her answers, however, and left the two men, telling Newman that he should let M. de Bellegarde know that if he wanted any information about her, he could get in from her.

When Newman expressed his disappointment to the old man, M. Nioche avowed that he did not approve of his daughter's behavior but that he had to tolerate it. Of course, he admitted that the girl had delivered money to him that day. Newman cautioned the old man not to hurt the girl and left.

A week later, Newman visited Valentin and confessed that he had been proved right (that the father would accept money from his daughter without complaint). Valentin was obviously taken by the girl, and Newman warned him not to get involved.

Three days after his last meeting with Madame de Bellegarde, Newman entered his apartment and found an invitation that Madame would be receiving guests at her home on the 27th. Newman was pleased and he placed the announcement in the corner of his mirror. When Valentin visited him that evening, he saw it too: it caused him to comment facetiously that Newman would meet all the blue-bloods that evening. He did tell him not to be offensive. Valentin, however, could not keep his conversation away from thoughts about Noémie. Obviously, he was in love, although he refused to admit it. Newman commanded him to stay away from the adventuress, but Valentin seemed caught. "Yes, she's a frightful little monster!" he said.

Comment:

At this point in the novel James has made his complete preparation of Mademoiselle Nioche and her father. The girl has become a blatant fortune

hunter and the supposedly devoted and concerned father has become the full parasite. The unfortunate aspect, however, to all this is Valentin's deeper and deeper involvement with Noémie. James is pausing briefly here before the next climactic chapters in the novel, but his plot is moving forward. In many respects, James is making his most poignant and damaging comment on the old aristocracy in showing that Valentin has been completely taken by the young, scheming climber, Noémie. See Comment after Chapter Nineteen.

A small item should be noted here: at the end of the chapter, Valentin warns Newman to watch himself and not be offensive at the party that the Bellegardes are giving. The warning is well-intended; it is not, however, received.

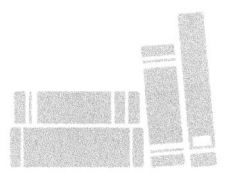

THE AMERICAN

TEXTUAL ANALYSIS

CHAPTERS 16 - 20

CHAPTER SIXTEEN

Newman was very happy during the next days. He never saw the old Madame de Bellegarde and the Marquis, because they were entertaining Lord Deepmere. Madame de Cintré herself was also very happy, and she tenderly scolded Newman for not giving her anything to scold him about and for idealizing her.

On the evening of the 27th Newman went a little early to the Bellegarde home on the Rue de l'Université. Madame de Bellegarde was dressed in purple and lace, Claire in white, and the Marquise in crimson crepe with huge silver moons bestrewn on her gown. As usual, she wanted to know Newman's reactions to her clothes. Claire did not speak to Newman as yet. Madame de Bellegarde, however, greeted him with "majestic formality" and introduced him in order to three dukes, three counts, and a baron. Lord Deepmere was there, laughing as usual.

Newman went over to the proper looking Marquis and asked him to introduce him to some of his friends. The Marquis walked through the reception rooms and escorted Newman to a lady obviously of importance, one could see, by the attitude that the Marquis held. The lady was "monumentally stout," had a triple chin, a "vast expanse of uncovered bosom," and an "immense circumference of satin petticoat." She reminded Newman of the Fat Lady at a fair, but Urbain was very respectful before her and formally introduced Newman to her. The fat duchess said that she had come to meet Newman and that she had heard the legends surrounding him. She mentioned such things as the city that Newman had founded, his fabulous wealth, and that he was going to be made president of America. Newman laughed out loud at all this, and several people turned to see who was laughing at the duchess. The Marquis then led Newman away, commenting that the duchess was "the greatest lady in France." Subsequently, he introduced the American to several more people, "selected apparently for their typically august character."

Newman found that he actually did wonder how he was conducting himself. He asked Mrs. Tristram, who came over to him after he had left the side of the Marquis, if he were holding his head too high. Newman escorted Mrs. Tristram through the rooms and presented her to Valentin. He left them together and looked for Madame de Bellegarde, whom he found eventually sitting in the first room with Lord Deepmere, both obviously engaged in serious conversation with Madame de Bellegarde awaiting an important answer. Lord Deepmere colored on seeing Newman. Newman apologized for interrupting, but Madame de Bellegarde said that she had been giving Lord Deepmere some advice and that it was up to him to take it.

Newman expressed pleasure at the party and asked Madame de Bellegarde to accompany him in a walk through the rooms.

The old lady accepted the invitation and walked with her hand on his arm beside him. When they reached the last room, she declared in a soft voice, "This is enough, sir," and went to the waiting outstretched hands of her son, the Marquis. Newman continued to find the party enjoyable, but he was glad when the guests started to leave.

Newman looked to speak to Claire for the first time in the evening. He finally found her in the conservatory off the garden with Lord Deepmere. As he approached, he heard Claire say to the nobleman, "It is almost a pity not to tell Mr. Newman." Once again, Lord Deepmere looked nervous on the arrival of Newman, but Claire did not refer to the topic of conversation she was having with her distant cousin. Newman wanted to know if Claire was satisfied with his behavior. She replied that she was very happy. As the two went inside, Mrs. Bread was there.

Comment:

In this very important chapter several significant incidents occur. In the later James novels, in scenes such as this one of the party of the Bellegardes, the novelist would handle his details very impressionistically, very vaguely, and allow the reader to draw his own conclusions. In **The American**, James is much more direct and specific, but the careless reader will lose many of the subtle implications that James has carefully prepared for.

> **To begin in order, one should note that James brings his American-in-Europe theme to a culminating point. Madame de Bellegarde introduces Newman to people in order of rank, but Newman is unperturbed. Then Urbain is careful to introduce his apparent future brother-in-law to the "greatest lady in France,"**

a fat, comical lady. The desperate urge of these people to think of Newman as a nobleman comes out in the decadent lady's legend surrounding the American: he has founded a city, he will be crowned king of the United States. Newman, injudiciously, perhaps ignorantly and vulgarly, certainly honestly and innocently, laughs right in the old, fat lady's face. It is a telling contrast, but a very poor point for Newman. He will pay for it later.

The second matter that one should note in the chapter occurs at two separate points and is resolved later in the novel. When Newman leaves Urbain, he seeks out Madame de Bellegarde. He finds her cornered with Lord Deepmere. The English distant cousin is openly embarrassed by Newman's arrival, but Madame de Bellegarde deftly says that she has advised her relative and it is up to him to act. Later in the evening, Newman comes upon Lord Deepmere with Claire, as they are discussing him. The American is so elated that he does not realize that Madame de Bellegarde has been intriguing against him and has asked Lord Deepmere to marry Claire. In Chapter Eighteen, after Newman finds that he cannot marry Claire, his confidante, Mrs. Tristram, will guess that the Bellegardes wanted Claire to marry Lord Deepmere. Newman will not believe it, but in his last meeting with Claire he will raise the point and she will admit that the proposal had been made to Lord Deepmere, but he had not wanted to participate in it. (In Chapter Twenty.)

The last item in the chapter is a seemingly more slight matter, but it has been considered by some people the climax of the novel, because it finally brings out the answer of Madame de Bellegarde which forms the heart of the novel. Newman is very pleased with the party. He asks Madame de Bellegarde to stroll through the rooms with him. Together they greet the guests, but after their march, Madame de Bellegarde much more upset than Newman can dream, says softly, "This is enough, sir." Later she tells Newman that it was at that point that she realized that she could not bear the thought of his marrying her daughter. There before all her friends, Madame de Bellegarde felt that she had fallen. It is a telling moment. Certainly, no one can blame Newman for not understanding the full import of her thoughts, but although the reader may violently oppose such rigidity, such seeming inhumanity, he must understand that so far as Madame de Bellegarde is concerned she is violating the world as she knows it. She cannot turn from this point, and the proof is that she does not.

CHAPTER SEVENTEEN

Newman liked music and attended the opera regularly. Two evenings after the affair at the Bellegardes he went to a performance of "Don Giovanni," an opera by Mozart. After the first act curtain Newman saw Urbain de Bellegarde and his wife, and decided to bid them good evening and leave. But as he looked around the theater, he saw Noémie Nioche in a box with a man he did not recognize. In the foyer of the theater Newman saw Valentin de Bellegarde, evidently lost in meditation. Newman asked what was the matter now, and Valentin told him that he was thinking of that "vulgar little wretch," meaning, of course, Mademoiselle Nioche. Newman was pleased that the Count now realized what kind of girl she actually was. Finally, the American suggested that Valentin allow him to find a place for him in America so that he could earn some money. He suggested a bank, a fitting place for Valentin, thought Newman. Valentin sounded somewhat interested and said that he needed a half hour of music to help him decide whether he could accept the offer.

In the meantime Newman dropped in to see the Marquis and Marquise. They discussed the opera very briefly, and the Marquis saw fit to leave. Madame de Bellegarde began asking Newman if he could arrange for her to see some of the different places in Paris that her husband did not approve of. When the curtain rose again, Newman returned to his seat.

Newman noticed that Valentin had settled in the box with Mademoiselle Nioche and her gentleman friend. During the next intermission, Newman questioned how much thinking Valentin could have accomplished in the box with that girl, but the Count told him that he was quite willing for Newman to find a place for him in America. Newman was pleased, but he saw that Valentin was ready to go back into the box with the woman and her friend. He tried to discourage his friend, but it was to no avail. Valentin explained that the box was not the gentleman's and that the man had come and occupied a place there while Valentin had left his place. Again Newman warned him to stay away from that woman.

During the next intermission, Newman approached the same box expecting to see Valentin again. Instead, he saw Valentin and the young man leave together. In the box, Noémie was openly pleased because she was sure that the men would have a duel over her. Newman was horrified. When the men returned, Valentin again insisted on entering the box against the judgment of Newman. Now Valentin informed his friend that he was indeed to have a duel with the gentleman, a Monsieur Stanislas Kapp, son and heir of a Strasbourg brewer. Later in the evening, after he had made the arrangements necessary, Valentin explained to the cynical Newman that the duel had to take place because it was a matter of honor not to accept an insult from another man, especially in the presence of a woman. Newman argued seriously that the whole thing was barbaric.

The next day, at dinner in Newman's apartment, Valentin revealed that the duel would take place in Geneva. Newman insisted on arguing with the French count, but Valentin was just as insistent that there was a matter of honor involved.

Comment:

The possible meanings of the duel between Valentin and Stanislas Kapp are discussed in the comment section following Chapter Nineteen. In preparation for that, however, James has moved considerably forward in his themes. The fact that Valentin is willing to accept the offer of going to work in America is a telling commentary on the aristocrats that the Bellegardes represent. Valentin, throughout the novel, has represented the decay of the aristocrats, but he has also represented the best of the figures because, like his sister, he is willing to attempt a break from the regimentation that his family background represents. It is unfortunate that he must be sacrificed, especially when one considers the low character of Noémie Nioche in the novel.

CHAPTER EIGHTEEN

The next morning Newman went to visit Madame de Cintré. Mrs. Bread told him, to his surprise, that the countess was going away and had left a message for him; Newman, excited, exclaimed, "Leaving town! What has happened?" Mrs. Bread explained that Claire was leaving for Fleurières, near Poitiers. The servant agreed to take Newman up to Claire's room.

Claire was standing in the middle of the room, Urbain was before the fireplace, and Madame de Bellegarde buried in an armchair. Newman went directly to Claire and asked her what was the matter. Claire, obviously distressed, answered, "Something grave has happened. I cannot marry you." She told him to ask her mother and brother why. Urbain simply said it was impossible; his mother echoed that it was all improper. Claire admitted that she had given up Newman. She was ashamed and she wanted only to be left alone.

Newman turned to the Marquis and stated that he thought the Marquis had given his word that he would not interfere. Urbain claimed that he had not interfered, nor had he attempted to persuade Claire. Newman, still at a loss, asked what they had done then. Urbain said that they had used "authority." "My mother commanded," said Claire. Newman now realized that they were making a distinction. He did not like it, but he understood. Madame de Bellegarde and her son explained their position. They explained that the match simply could not be tolerated by them. The old lady added that they had tried to accept Newman, but they were wrong. The party on Thursday evening proved it to her. "We really cannot reconcile ourselves to a commercial person," she said.

Newman insisted that he would follow Claire and speak to her, but Madame de Bellegarde was confident that the daughter had given her word and would not break it. Urbain told Newman that it would be a "silly waste of money" for him to go to Poitiers after Claire.

Newman left the house. He felt a deep "personal outrage." He strolled about the city, deeply upset. Finding himself near the house of Mrs. Tristram, he went in to see her and told her the new circumstances. When he finished the story, she said, "They want her to marry Lord Deepmere." Newman would hear none of that. He sat a while longer and then went back to his apartment, where there was a telegram from Valentin asking him to come to Geneva because he, Valentin, was seriously ill. Newman had to defer his intention of following Claire and pleading his case with her, but he wrote her a short note explaining that he did not give up yet and that he intended to see her soon. Then he caught a night express to Geneva.

Comment:

Newman is totally unprepared for the shock he receives in the chapter. In his way of looking at things, he has assumed that the marriage must go through because he has been accepted by Claire who loves him. He has assumed that the Bellegardes, especially after the party given in his honor, have learned to accept him. Psychologically, he is in no way prepared for the final statement that the marriage is "impossible" and "improper."

> First, one must examine the behavior of the Bellegardes. According to Urbain's way of thinking, he and his mother have lived by the letter of their promise to Newman that they would not interfere with his courting of Claire. They have allowed him his due, and they have allowed Claire to make her

decision. At this point, they are saying that they do not accept her decision. They have used, as Urbain puts it, authority. They have, as Claire puts it, commanded. The distinction is a fine one, but it is a problem because Newman has assumed that the Bellegardes would act honestly, or better put, act as he would. He has failed to realize how far they would go to protect their tradition and their family. At the necessary point, if there is a choice to be made between morality and the preservation of the established order of the old world, the Bellegardes, sterile, withdrawn from the world, decaying, and lonely, must still according to their own code choose their social world. It is unfair for the open and innocent nature of Newman to be exposed to the traditions of another world on these terms, but these are the terms and he is the victim.

How does one explain the behavior of Claire? Claire has made a commitment to the family that she will abide by their decisions after she had not fought for the fortune of Monsieur de Cintré. If that is not enough, one must also realize that the choice for Claire is much more complicated than it is for Newman. She must choose what her family represents and what its entire world represents, or she must choose to abandon all else for the man she loves. As the reader finds out very shortly, Claire cannot choose her family any longer, but she cannot selfishly choose to run away from the world that they represent. She does commit herself to a tradition that is much more severe and much more telling than the rules of the aristocracy when she joins the religious order of the Carmelites. Claire makes it clear that she wants Newman, but she cannot break from the family. She cannot live in the world without Newman; so she chooses to leave the world for the sanctuary of the convent.

The rejection of Newman is the climax of the novel. What is left is to see how he behaves once the clash between what he represents and what the Bellegardes represent has occurred.

CHAPTER NINETEEN

Newman sat still on the train trip, his eyes shut so that one looking at him would think he was asleep. He did not sleep except for two hours and then got off the train about half an hour before Geneva. He was met at the station by a man who told him that Valentin was dying and a priest had seen him the previous evening. He was now being attended to by a companion, a M. de Grosjoyaux. Newman's new companion explained that on the first round of the duel, Valentin had grazed the arm of Kapp, while the latter had missed completely. But the beer baron, not one to live by the best noble traditions of the match, demanded a second round. Valentin fired to miss, but Kapp mortally wounded the Count.

At the inn, Valentin was asleep, and Mr. Ledoux, Valentin's second, announced a moving eulogy for the nobility of the wounded person, but Newman was not in the mood to be good company. Newman lay down for a time; then he wandered about the Alpine village. The doctor later gave him permission to sit by Valentin's bed. While he was sitting there, the dying count awoke, made some typically facetious remarks, and asked after his sister. Newman explained that his sister had left Paris for their château and that he had not seen Valentin's mother and brother.

Valentin was disappointed, but he noticed Newman's face and realized that something was wrong between him and Claire. Newman told Valentin not to be concerned with that now and only by getting better would he be of any help to him, Newman, and Claire. Valentin was quiet for a time, and then he apologized for not being able to take the bank position that Newman would have arranged. "I might have become another Rothschild," he said.

Although the doctor did not like it because Newman was the only one who excited Valentin, he allowed the American to be with the Count again that evening. Valentin knew that he was right in the morning. There was something between Claire and Newman. Newman told him the truth, that Madame de Bellegarde and Urbain had stopped the marriage. Valentin was ashamed and he apologized for his family. The doctor, at this point, knew Valentin was failing, but the dying man demanded five more private minutes with Newman.

Then Valentin told Newman that there was an "immense secret" that could be used against his mother and brother. Both of them knew it, and it concerned the death of his father. Valentin, failing badly, finally revealed that Newman could get the secret from Mrs. Bread. "It will avenge you," he murmured feebly.

Comment:

The death of Valentin de Bellegarde serves in the plot of the novel. That can be turned to in a few moments. The meanings of his death are much more significant when one thinks of them as a commentary on the whole problem of the aristocrats and the Europeans in the novel. It has been obvious throughout that Valentin has been trying to break away from the restrictions of his family background. He has held a "moral grudge" against the family. Although he has been properly schooled, he has tried to remain an individual, but he has been criticized by the family. Then the reader has seen Valentin attracted to the very common and disreputable Noémie Nioche. On her account, moreover, he has fought a mortal duel with a new upstart businessman, an heir to a brewer's fortune. It is the Bellegarde in him that kills him. It is his senseless - Newman thinks it barbaric - desire to live by the code of the nobleman and defend the honor of a useless fortune-hunter. This is the most ironic moment in the novel. It is probably, by extension, Henry James's most severe criticism of the world that Newman, the American, cannot understand at all.

In terms of the plot of the novel, the revelation of Valentin to Newman that there is an "immense secret" in the family background that will give Newman a chance to take revenge on the Bellegardes is pure melodrama. The dying man's revealing statement is almost too, too obvious a device that the later James, as a novelist, would never indulge in. As he himself said, however, he had here a romance.

CHAPTER TWENTY

Valentin de Bellegarde died the next morning, and Newman left in an hour because he did not want to see Madame de Bellegarde and her son. He wrote the details of the tragic affair to Claire and asked her for word when he could see her. He received a short note that Valentin would be buried at the family château at Fleurières.

Newman stayed in the background at the funeral and three days later sent a note to Claire that he wanted to see her. He went to the massive castle and was shown in to a large room to wait for Madame de Cintré. Claire, dressed in black, entered from another room. She thanked him for his thoughtfulness, but told him that nothing could come of their meeting because everything was decided. Newman could not understand why Claire should fear her mother. It was her conscience that made her feel her mother's demands, she said. Newman knew that Claire would not leave him for Lord Deepmere, as Madame de Bellegarde would like. Claire was surprised Newman had understood this, but this was not the point at all.

Newman pleaded still. The whole thing had hurt him deeply. Striking his heart, he said, "And what I feel here is a glowing fire!" At this Claire tried to explain herself: "It's like a religion. There is a curse upon the house.... I have been selfish; I wanted to escape from it. You offered me a great chance - besides my liking you.... But I can't - it has overtaken and come back to me." She sobbed as she spoke, her composure gone.

Then Claire told Newman that she was going to enter a Carmelite convent to become a nun. Newman could not stand the idea of her "behind locks and bars." He begged her not to go through with it. She said, it was all decided: "Do you suppose I will go on living in the world, still beside you, and yet not with you?"

Newman took her into his arms, held her close, and kissed her white face. "For an instant she resisted, and for a moment she submitted; then, with a force, she disengaged herself and hurried away." Newman left.

> Comment:

This is the last meeting between Claire and Newman, and it is the only speech that Henry James allows his heroine to make in defense of her final decision. Much of the previous commentary has attempted to explain Claire's position.

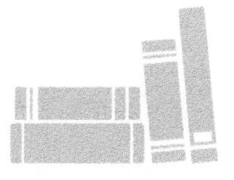

THE AMERICAN

TEXTUAL ANALYSIS

CHAPTERS 21 - 26

CHAPTER TWENTY-ONE

Newman walked around the town of Poitiers, full of thoughts about the whole situation. He found himself incapable of walking away from the injury that he had suffered. "Now his sense of outrage was deep, rancorous, and ever present; he felt that he was a good fellow wronged." He really could not understand the thoughts of Claire. He remembered the way she looked and the things she said, but any way he thought of it, he still came to the conclusion that they must have used force against her.

On the next day he decided to go to the château. He wanted to give Madame de Bellegarde and her son one more opportunity to change their minds. When he arrived at the house, which struck him as a "horrible rubbish-heap of iniquity," he met Mrs. Bread, who as usual knew what had transpired. She informed him that Madame de Cintré had left for Paris to join a Carmelite order of nuns that morning and had told her mother and brother the night before. Mrs. Bread then asked about Valentin's last moments, and Newman took the opportunity to ask her to meet him that evening at dusk in the court before the nearby church so that he might relate something to her that Valentin had said. Mrs. Bread agreed.

Newman was then led into the large drawing-room where the Marquis and his mother were. Both had looks of deep worry. Newman wasted almost no time and asked them to free Claire. He felt that they should want very much to stop their daughter and sister from entering a convent, but Urbain made it clear that they preferred that to her marrying Newman. Then Newman quite stunned the two people present when he told them that Valentin on his death bed expressed shame for them and apologized for their behavior. Both were incredulous, but they obviously were deeply affected by the statement. Madame de Bellegarde was insulted and left the room.

When Newman was alone with the Marquis, he sprang his statement. "You have a secret - you have a skeleton in the closet," he said. He continued, "You and your mother have committed a crime." Newman could see that the Marquis was profoundly startled. The American told the truth, but he pressed his point by threatening to find out the whole story and then reveal it if Urbain and his mother did not free Claire. He gave the Marquis until three o'clock that afternoon to send an answer. Although Newman expected no reply, he received an answer in the form of a note telling him that the Bellegardes were returning to Paris to confirm Claire's resolve to take religious vows.

That evening Newman kept his appointment with Mrs. Bread.

> Comment:

Beginning with this chapter to the end of the novel, one might think of the rest of the novel as a "test for Christopher Newman." There are two points in his mind as the chapter opens. First, he still thinks that he can get Claire back. Second, he is bent on satisfying himself by hurting the Bellegardes. It is this second aspect of these last chapters that will give Newman a chance to live up to the character that he has been in the novel and before the reader has met him.

Of course, he hurts the Bellegardes when he tells them that Valentin apologized for them on his death bed. But he gets the response he is looking for when he sees Urbain's reactions to his statement that he knows there is a family secret.

CHAPTER TWENTY-TWO

Newman and Mrs. Bread sat on some rocks in the churchyard. First, Newman wanted to know what they, Urbain and Madame de Bellegarde, had done to Claire. Mrs. Bread said, "They worked on her feelings; they knew that was the way. She is a delicate creature. They made her feel wicked. She is only too good." Eventually, Claire gave in because she was afraid of what she might know about her mother.

Newman wanted to turn to that point. Mrs. Bread was reluctant at first, but Newman vowed that the last thing that Valentin told him was to ask Mrs. Bread. The old lady intimated that the information would destroy the family and that she was concerned. When Newman told her that she was to fond of her mistress, Mrs. Bread responded with the fact that she had held a grudge for many years against Madame de Bellegarde. It seemed that many years ago, Madame de Bellegarde in a fit of jealousy had accused Mrs. Bread of trying to attract her husband with a red ribbon in her hair. Mrs. Bread had kept that ribbon all these years.

Mrs. Bread was quiet for a time, and Newman waited. Eventually, she began her long story about the death of the old Marquis de Bellegarde. The Marquis was an old man, and two years after the marriage of Urbain, Madame de Bellegarde had decided to marry Claire off to the old Monsieur de Cintré. The Marquis was violently opposed to the marriage because he favored Claire. After a violent quarrel with Madame de Bellegarde, the old Marquis took seriously ill. At first it looked as if he would die and two Paris doctors gave up on him, but a local doctor tended to him until the old Marquis looked as if he would survive. The doctor gave him a medicine that stopped the stomach pains that were killing the old man.

Mrs. Bread said that the Marquise was obviously disappointed in the better condition of her husband. One evening while Mrs. Bread was with the Marquis, Madame de Bellegarde and Urbain came to his room and insisted that Mrs. Bread leave. Mrs. Bread did not undress and saw fit to return to the room much later. When she got there, Madame de Bellegarde and Urbain announced that the Marquis was dead. Urbain left for a doctor in Poitiers, and later Madame de Bellegarde left the room to greet him on his return.

Mrs. Bread went near the bed of the Marquis with a candle, and to her near shock, she saw that the Marquis was alive. The old man groaned that his wife had murdered him. Suddenly, he asked for pencil and paper, which Mrs. Bread got for him. Painfully, he wrote something down and gave the paper to Mrs.

Bread and told her to give it to someone who would use it. A little later Urbain entered the room and announced that a doctor would be coming. The doctor, when he did come, ministered to the sick man and kept him alive, but the old Marquis died the next day.

Newman immediately asked about the note, but Mrs. Bread, who could not read it because it was in French, said that no one had seen it till that day. She said that there was some talk on the death of the Marquis, but it did not amount to much. The servant conjectured that Madame de Bellegarde participated in causing the death by refusing to give medicine to her husband when he needed it.

Newman escorted the lady back to the château. She entered by a side door and returned in half an hour with the note and handed it to Newman. The American promised to take care of her and returned to the inn. With the French he was able to learn from M. Nioche, he translated the note, which said that Madame de Bellegarde had on that evening murdered her husband. The note was signed by the old Marquis.

Comment:

The story of the death of the old Marquis de Bellegarde speaks for itself. Mrs. Bread gets her say in the novel. It is this function that has caused critics to refer to her presence as being mechanical in the novel.

What is important, however, is the revelation of the capability of evil that resides in the aloof and distant aristocracy. In the way that the death of the father is revealed, one realizes that James is telling us that

Madame de Bellegarde and Urbain did what they did so that they could marry off Claire as they pleased. It is with this point that one realizes the horror of the entire story. The skeleton is there, but the reflection on the living is horrible.

An interesting note here: one critical article on the novel, written some years ago, stressed the fact that Madame de Bellegarde insisted on the marriage of Claire to the old Monsieur de Cintré because she was having an affair with the old man. It is ingenious.

CHAPTER TWENTY-THREE

The second day after his conversation with Mrs. Bread, Newman returned to Paris. He called at the home of the Bellegardes, and was told that they had returned from Poitiers, but he decided against seeing them for a time. He went home and had just stretched his legs out when his servant announced Mrs. Bread.

The servant was dressed in her best attire with a bonnet. Newman greeted her warmly and assured her that he had not at all forgotten his proposal that she come work for him. She informed Newman that Claire had refused to see her brother and mother at the convent. Soon her chance to see anyone would be over, Mrs. Bread informed Newman. The Carmelites were strict, the lady continued, and "they go off to cold places to pray to the Virgin Mary." "The Virgin Mary is a hard mistress," she commented. Newman found from her that there were two Carmelite convents and Claire was in one on the Avenue de Messine. After that conversation, Newman asked Mrs. Bread to choose any room she liked for herself.

The next day Mrs. Bread returned after telling Madame de Bellegarde that she was leaving her service with her and going to Newman's. Madame de Bellegarde was quite upset by the departure and Newman took it to mean that she was "scared."

Newman had not shown Mrs. Tristram the letter he had, but he had seen her several times since his return to Paris. He was greatly disappointed in his affairs and took no pains to hide it from Mrs. Tristram, who in her turn was thinking of repairing the hurt to the American by finding someone else for him. Newman, however, wanted no more of that; instead, he asked her if she could get him into the Carmelite monastery. Mrs. Tristram was happy to have something to do for him.

Comment:

Mrs. Bread's quick arrival at the quarters of Newman is a brief but sure insight into the mind of the devoted domestic. She comes ready to serve her new master, once she has divested herself of the note and has fulfilled her service to Madame de Bellegarde. At the end of the novel, all of Newman's apartment, its lavish, gilded rooms, will be hers to clean, to move the dust from one place to another, for Newman knows that he will never return.

CHAPTER TWENTY-FOUR

On Sunday Newman went to the Carmelite convent, with the single hope of seeing Claire. He went into the chapel and waited until the mass started. He could not understand the genuflections and the chants. In the middle of the mass, from behind a screen, suddenly Newman heard the wail of the nuns, a seeming dirge to Newman's ears, the only sound that the nuns made in their religious lives. Newman thought it was horrible and hideous as it continued, and he thought he could hear the voice of Claire among the many other voices. He rose abruptly and left the chapel.

On the way out, he saw Madame de Bellegarde and her son talking to the same sister who had admitted him. The three recognized each other, but Newman was intent on getting out beyond the walls of the stifling convent. Outside, he saw the young Marquise de Bellegarde sitting in a landau. She commented that he looked as if he had seen a ghost. He answered, "I have!" After some brief talk, Newman assumed that the young Marquise would be waiting for her husband and his mother and asked her to do him the favor of returning a little late so that he might have a chance to talk to them. She informed him that she was to meet them in a nearby park and that he could have a better opportunity there.

Finally, Madame de Bellegarde and her son came to the park. Newman stood in their way and said he had something to tell them. Quite directly, he addressed the old dowager Marquise, "You killed your husband." She at first feigned nonchalance, but when Newman said that he had a signed document, Madame de Bellegarde sat on a bench, her face distorted by agitation.

Newman handed a copy of the original to Urbain, who read it and stared at it. He told them that he would start by showing it to the duchess he had met at their party. Madame de Bellegarde assumed that he had gotten the information from Mrs. Bread, whom she referred to as "my husband's mistress." The old lady turned to her son, "My son, say something," she said. Urbain answered, "What shall I say?" Then the mother said, "Mon pauvre ami" (my poor dear) and asked to be taken to the carriage. As she left, Newman said to himself, "Damn it, she is plucky!"

Newman expected to hear from them soon, but not so soon as the next morning when Urbain did call. At first, the Marquis admitted that they thought the document to be genuine, as he pout it. He continued that only for the respect of his father did they want the document. Of course, Newman laughed at this. Urbain admitted that the duchess (Madame d'Outreville) would be shocked by the information. Newman asked what the Marquis was actually proposing. The marquis answered, "What we offer you is a chance - a chance that a gentleman should appreciate." Newman responded that what he wanted was Claire, but the nobleman would hear none of that. Finally, the meeting was over.

Comment:

The chapter has three parts to it and all three are major steps to the final resolution of the novel. The first is perhaps the most profoundly disturbing part of the novel. Newman goes to the Carmelite convent. Protestant that he is, a not very religious man in the orthodox sense, a man who raced through four hundred seventy cathedrals during his grand tour of Europe, Newman is uncomfortable and ill at ease during the Catholic mass. He does not understand the symbolic acts of the people participating in the service, just as he has not understood one bit the behavior of the Europeans he has been involved with. Then Newman thinks he can distinguish the voice of Claire among the wailing voices behind the screen. The screen is forbidding, for it too is a convention that is a part of the whole pattern of things that Newman has not been able to understand. Of course, the deep irony of the scene is that Claire is not a part of the wailing and horrible chorus at all. When Newman leaves the convent and hears the young Marquise de Bellegarde exclaim that he looked as if he had seen a ghost, and he replies that he had, the pitiful end of his majestic desire to marry his ideal woman, the crowning glory of his career, is at an end.

The second part of the chapter is the direct confrontation between Newman and the Bellegardes in the park. Newman stuns the mother and son. Madame de Bellegarde, agitated though she may be, still retains her poise and her dignity. She asks to leave, but she makes her single and only defense when she says that Mrs. Bread, from whom Newman got the incriminating letter, was her husband's mistress. Madame de Bellegarde remains strong. Her son, however, is immobilized. He does not know how to act. He looks to his mother to do something and to say something. Urbain is reduced by Newman, completely reduced to the mother's son, a character without a personality.

The final part of the chapter is Urbain's visit to Newman. It is the final meeting. The American and the Europeans have never been so far apart, but Urbain's plea, that Newman use the opportunity as a gentleman would, is telling.

CHAPTER TWENTY-FIVE

Newman called on the comical, fat duchess, Madame d'Outreville, and found her at home. He entered her apartment and an old gentleman took leave. Later an Italian prince called. Newman listened to the chatter of the duchess, and then it dawned on him, a "sudden sense of the folly of his errand." He asked himself why he was there to expose the Bellegardes and what real difference it would make. Abruptly, he rose from his place and bade good-bye.

Newman tried not to think of the Bellegardes. He dined with the Tristrams, and Tom turned to the subject. He blamed his wife for the whole affair. Mrs. Tristram tried to defend herself. Newman asked her if she thought that he actually would succeed. She said she did, "But, it was the highest flight ever taken by a tolerably bold imagination." She recommended that Newman leave Paris for some time.

In a short time, the American went to London and found himself enjoying the city in comparison to Paris. One day in Hyde Park, among a crowd of women he saw Mademoiselle Nioche being escorted by a well-dressed gentleman. Newman sat down on a bench and realized after a time that he was next to, of all people, M. Nioche. The embarrassed old man continued to deprecate his daughter's behavior and claim that he would do something about it, but Newman knew the truth and told the old man that he was doing a good job following Noémie. A little later, the daughter came to the bench with her gentleman, who proved to be Lord Deepmere. Lord Deepmere had met the adventuress in Paris, and knew that she was at the bottom of Valentin's duel and death. Newman pulled away from the three people. M. Nioche whispered in his ear that someday Newman would read about his actions in the paper, but Newman never did read the sequel.

Comment:

Newman's disgust at himself for being at the home of the duchess is preparation for the final chapter. He realizes that nothing he can do will change the way of life that the duchess and the Bellegardes lead.

Newman is of course disgusted with Noémie, her father, and Lord Deepmere.

CHAPTER TWENTY-SIX

Newman remained in England for a time, but no matter how he tried to distract himself, his thoughts always came back to one point. From England he traveled back to New York. From New York he went to San Francisco. His own indifference at the stock market troubled him, but he could not gather any enthusiasm. He returned to New York, and toward the end of winter he received a letter from Mrs. Tristram in which she wrote that a few days before Claire de Cintré had taken the veil of a Carmelite nun and the name of Sister Veronica.

That night, Newman took a steamship back to France. Mrs. Bread, keeping a lonely vigil at his apartment, was glad to see him. He told her that he was back for good. He found that Claire was now in the convent on Rue d'Enfer. He walked about the city and came to the section where the convent was. He stood across the street and he realized that those walls were the reason for his trip. He walked away and entered a church. He did not pray. He just sat there and somewhere in his thoughts realized that the Bellegardes still existed, but he was sorry for what he meant to do. He resolved against it.

He returned to his apartment and told Mrs. Bread to pack for him because he would never return again. Late in the evening he went to the Tristrams. Tom decided to leave him with his wife. After a few words, Newman took out the note that he had carried with him. He said he intended to burn up the Bellegardes for good. He told Mrs. Tristram that the note contained a secret that could destroy the Bellegardes. He tossed the paper into the fire. Mrs. Tristram asked him if the information had humbled the Bellegardes. Newman said that it did not. Then Mrs. Tristram thought aloud and surmised, "Their confidence, after counsel taken of each other, was not in their innocence, nor in their talent for bluffing things off; it was in your remarkable good nature! You see they were right."

Instinctively, Newman turned to look for the paper, but there was nothing left of it.

Comment:

Henry James gave his hero one more opportunity, and Newman lived up to the highest ideals in his character. The novel comes to a close only after Newman has returned to stare at the walls of the convent. Claire is now housed in the one on the Rue d'Enfer (translation of the French word: hell, or torment). He is then filled with disgust for what he wanted to do to the Bellegardes. When Newman burns the note, he is proving the gentleman that the nobility can never be because of their past. Of course, Mrs. Tristram is right when she says that the Bellegardes had counted on Newman's "remarkable good nature." But Mrs. Tristram has also made the best summary of the quest of Newman for the ideal beauty of Claire in Chapter Twenty-five: "It was the highest flight ever taken by a tolerably bold imagination."

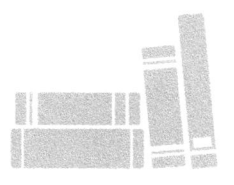

THE AMERICAN

CHARACTER ANALYSES

CHRISTOPHER NEWMAN

The American is about Christopher Newman. Christopher Newman is the American. With his symbolic name, the "new" man, the American arrives in Europe. He has been successful, extraordinarily successful, in business, and at a particular point in his career, a certain nobility and decency in him have caused him to turn away in disgust from a business transaction with which he could have hurt another man who had wronged him previously. He is "intensely Western," self-made, self-confident. He has an "esthetic headache" from the art he has been looking at in the famous museum of the Louvre. From the very beginning one can see that he is not in Europe for culture. He will do most of the typically American things, but he will also remain an individual. Newman is then a composite portrait of the new American man. He represents at all turns in the novel those things that are distinctly American.

When Mrs. Tristram tells him about Claire de Cintré, Newman reveals that he has many reasons for being in Europe, but there is one over-riding thought in his mind. Newman wants a wife, a woman who will culminate his very successful life, a "statue on top of a monument." That wife will be Claire de Cintré, he decides. With that one decision, Newman, with his self-assurance, his candor, his directness, his innocence, and his freedom, places himself directly in contrast to a society that is completely different from anything he knows. He is an intruder. As one critic puts it, he is a man without traditions and antecedents placed in a society that cherishes those things as if they were life itself. Newman lives as he knows and he is willing to accept the restrictions that the French family, the Bellegardes, put on him. He almost wins his prize, his ideal woman, but the noble people are in reality treacherous and they tell him that they cannot accept him because he is "too commercial."

It is when Newman is rejected by the Bellegardes that his true character has an opportunity to assert itself. At first, Newman, wounded and hurt, deprived of his love, wants revenge. Then he is given the important piece of evidence that he can use against the Bellegardes. At first, he is willing to use that evidence, but after he thinks of these decadent people, their sterile and useless lives, he realizes that if he were to reveal the evil of the Bellegardes, nothing would really occur in the patterns and institutions that have denied him his goddess. Newman is disgusted with himself. He decides not to reveal the secret, and he retains his decency and self-respect. In the end, as Henry James himself says, Newman is a magnanimous figure. He is also noble.

Henry James has drawn Christopher Newman quite completely in the novel. Actually, he is the center of the novel. However, there are some questions in the reader's mind at the end. Does Newman ever realize the violent assault he has made on the traditions of his adversaries? Does Newman realize what Claire has done in choosing to reject her family and in giving herself over to another old world institution, the religious order? Is Newman a changed man at the end of the novel? The answer to all these questions is probably, "No."

MADAME DE BELLEGARDE

The dowager head of the Bellegarde household is a formidable adversary for Newman. She is a very strong character, and a failure to understand her is a failure to understand the novel. Madame de Bellegarde is cruel, shrewd, and wise. She is the embodiment of the society that Newman is trying to conquer. From the very first meeting, Madame de Bellegarde treats him with condescension, almost with disdain. She is willing to accept the American, however distasteful it is to her, however dangerous it is to her life, probably only because of his enormous wealth. When Newman wants to give a party to announce his engagement, Madame de Bellegarde refuses to be outdone and asserts her ancient prerogative of giving a party first, although she cannot afford it. It is at that very engagement party when the upstart American has paraded her before her friends that Madame de Bellegarde realizes that the marriage of her daughter to the American is "impossible" and "improper." She realizes, as Newman cannot, how much of a threat he really is. He is sounding a death knell to her entire way of life, to her traditions, to her accepted proprieties. Without apologies that she is embarrassed to hear her son deliver, Madame de Bellegarde is willing to reject the monies and wealth of Newman to preserve her own society. As Newman himself prophetically says early in the novel to his confidante, Mrs. Tristram, she is a woman who could commit murder for a cause.

As many readers of the novel have commented, Madame de Bellegarde and her son are too sharply and directly drawn by

Henry James. Many have questioned the necessity of having her participate in the murder of her husband, but the reader must realize that James has drawn a strong and persistent character in Madame de Bellegarde. It is she who supports her institutions and defeats the assault on them.

URBAIN DE BELLEGARDE, THE MARQUIS

At first, Urbain de Bellegarde seems a complete character. He embodies, like his mother, the characteristics of the aristocracy that he so strongly supports. He is formal, proper, cold. On his first meeting with Newman, he refuses to shake hands. He speaks to him condescendingly and finds it difficult to explain how much adjusting the family must do to the idea of his sister's marrying a common businessman. But the reader slowly realizes that the haughty and proper Urbain is a lifeless mannequin. He seems a character in his own right, but early in the novel, Newman comments to himself that the Marquis is the mother at second hand. At the point of crisis for the Bellegardes, when Newman shows them the copy of the signed document which incriminates both mother and son, Urbain de Bellegarde is left immobile and frozen. He does not know what to say, so he turns to his mother, who simply refers to him as "my poor dear." The Marquis is a puppet for his mother. His actions are dictated, more so than his mother's, by how his society tells him to act. He has no self, no character.

VALENTIN DE BELLEGARDE

The younger of the two Bellegarde brothers represents another aspect of the aristocracy. He has tried to be a rebel from the strictures and **conventions** of his mother's and brother's society.

He holds a "moral grudge" against family discipline because it has not given him an opportunity to become a person and a useful figure. He befriends Newman early, and much of his delight seems to come from seeing the family upset. In championing Newman, he seems to be an example of the possibility of some hope for the decadent state of the aristocratic lives. Valentin's aristocratic background and its now useless institutions finally catch up with Valentin when he is brought to death because he is willing to defend the honor of a cheap fortune-hunter. This is James's most ironic thrust in the novel. The institution of the duel kills Valentin. In a certain sense, Valentin died when he criticized and apologized for his family's behavior, or he died, so far as the world of the Bellegardes is concerned, when he decided to take a position in a bank in America. Of course, the family never knew that, but one wonders what they would have said.

MADAME CLAIRE DE CINTRÉ

The American student finds it very hard to understand the character of Claire as Henry James presents her. For example, it would seem easy for her to marry Newman and leave France and her family and live happily ever after, many students say. There are reasons for these thoughts, and some of them seem valid. Many critics have felt that Henry James did not develop the character of Madame de Cintré fully enough. To a great extent that is true, but there are more reasons to believe that such criticism is not valid.

One must begin by remembering that Claire has had a short, tragic, and humiliating marriage that her family arranged. She has turned herself over to that same family because she was unwilling to contest the will of her old, evil husband. Then

Newman comes to her, proposes suddenly, and presents an opportunity to free herself of her family. Claire accepts. One must understand that she loves Newman deeply and completely. She is willing to give up her family and the world she has known for him. One cannot measure love any more significantly than that. However, Claire is willing to reject Newman at the command and authority of her family. It is the choice between love and **convention**. Claire must choose convention if she is to go beyond herself.

Claire directly says to Newman that she cannot remain in the world without him, but she cannot choose him against the will of her family. The depth of her love comes out when one realizes that, since she cannot have Newman, she chooses to give up the world for the institution of the convent. Of course, Newman cannot ever understand this. Claire has chosen a much deeper tradition than her family.

MRS. TRISTRAM

The lady who has many beginnings in her life that come to nothing serves as the confidante for Newman. James uses her to evaluate items for Newman. She has some insight into the problems in Newman's life. For example, she realizes that the family wants to marry Claire to Lord Deepmere. She also realizes that the Bellegardes counted on Newman's good nature to stop him from exposing them.

NOÉMIE NIOCHE

The young, pretty French girl is an adventuress, as Newman says, and a fortune-hunter. She does not realize that the shrewd businessman, Newman, sees through her overcharging him for her poor paintings. She is immoral, and it is through her involvement with Valentin that James is able to get his ironic twist of comment on the aristocrats. Her love affairs are a direct contrast to the love of Newman and Claire.

OTHER CHARACTERS

There are other minor characters who can be briefly cited: M. Nioche, the father of the fortune-hunter, who claims that he will kill his daughter for her immorality but who becomes a parasite on her new money; the young Marquise de Bellegarde, Urbain's wife, who is always concerned with her dresses and who finally tries to help Newman; the Reverend Benjamin Babcock, the Unitarian minister from Massachusetts, who cannot tolerate Newman's epicurean desire for pleasure on his European trip and who leaves a contrast to Newman in the reader's mind with his rigid moralistic tone; Madame Dandelard, the noble woman, who entertains people in her apartment with stories of the beatings that she has taken from her husband; Lord Deepmere, the distant cousin of the Bellegardes, who will not participate in the plot to marry Claire, but who laughs at the death of Valentin and takes up with Mlle. Nioche; Stanislas Kapp, the beer baron, who kills Valentin without observing the rules of gentlemen; Madame d'Outreville, the fat and comical duchess, who is the "greatest lady in France" and into whose ridiculous face Newman laughs; Mrs. Bread, the devoted domestic who has kept the secret of the Bellegardes and who reveals it to Newman, and who still keeps the red ribbon that the old Marquis once complimented; Madame Rochfidele, who looks over Newman through antique glasses and wonders how one approaches an American; and Monsieur Rochfidele, who knows how to speak to an American because he remembers Dr. Franklin from the previous century.

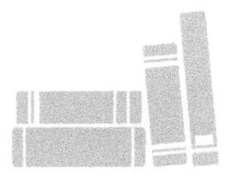

THE AMERICAN

CRITICAL COMMENTARY

Henry James has been the subject of intense critical attention and commentary for the last fifty years, and there are no signs that the books on James will cease in the near future. *The American*, like many of James's novels, has received attention because it was a definite success when it first appeared in 1877. The following section, beginning with Henry James's own comments, summarizes the best opinions on the novel. The student who wishes to go further in his study should consult the basic works cited in the Selected Bibliography and pay special attention to the essay by Oscar Cargill discussed below.

HENRY JAMES'S "PREFACE" TO "THE AMERICAN"

From 1907 to 1917 Charles Scribner's brought out a collected edition of the works of Henry James. These volumes are referred to as "The New York Edition." For each of the works James wrote a Preface in which he detailed the sources of the work, his techniques, and his particular problems in writing the story. The Preface to *The American* is a particularly extensive one, and it gives much insight to the special emphases and ideas that the author thought of in the novel. Among other things, some of the important elements of the preface are as follows: Henry James says he began the novel early in the winter of 1875-1876. He says that he enjoyed the subject, the idea attracted him. He recalls that he was in an American "horse-car" when the subject of the story first came to him. He wondered what a compatriot, meaning an American, would do after he had been cruelly wronged or betrayed in another, aristocratic society. The people of that society would have to be in every way superior to him. His American would have to behave in a "most interesting manner." He would be badly hurt, and he would harbor his feelings of revenge, but he would let his betrayers go. He would not forgive them, but at the end of the novel all he would have left would be his "moral necessity" of his "unappreciated magnanimity." The man at the end with his willingness not to use his strength was what James was working for, he says. That was his subject.

Once he found Christopher Newman, James continues, he experienced no difficulty. Then he had to decide on the "affront" the hero had to suffer. He did not want him "jilted." No, he wanted the heroine to suffer as much. It was at this point that the author realized that he was plotting a "romance." At this point James goes through a long digression on the meanings and implications of the term romance. He says that some of the things in the novel he fashioned not as they actually were, but as they fit his idea. For example, he cites the house of the Bellegardes. Another example is most interesting: he says that the Bellegardes in real life would have jumped at the opportunity of the money of the "rich and easy American."

James later in the Preface does not apologize for the romantic aspect of his novel. He says that what really mattered in the novel was the consistency in the character of Christopher Newman. It was he who had to be maintained as the "centre" in the story. James explains that he made extensive revisions of the original story for the New York Edition. He particularly cites the difficulty in making Claire recede from the scene after Madame de Bellegarde had introduced Newman to her friends and still maintain her (Claire's) character as important in the novel. James admits that he might have been wrong in thinking that Newman could bear the entire weight of the novel from that point on. Finally, he says, the novel must stand as it is.

OSCAR CARGILL, "THE NOVELS OF HENRY JAMES"

In this work, which is one of the most intelligent and outstanding studies of the works of Henry James, Oscar Cargill reviews almost every important study of the novel. The documentation alone is a veritable compendium of the best thoughts on *The American*. Cargill traces most of the ground that has been covered and adds his own important comments on the critical attitudes that one may hold on the novel. The author begins by tracing the background of *The American* thoroughly. He points out that James began the novel in 1875 when he was settled in Paris. He goes on to cite the influence of the Russian novelist, Ivan Turgenev. The next influence is a very interesting one, for it seems to parallel *The American* so closely. Professor Cargill cites an essay that discusses the works of a playwright Émile Augier and his persistent "intrusion" plot. That plot consisted of an intruder and a group and the resultant conflict, with one party's eyes being opened. Of course, Newman would be the intruder and the Bellegardes the group. Next, Cargill raises another interesting point. In 1876 James attended a play entitled *L'Étrangère* by Alexandre Dumas, fils. An American foreigner is highly criticized in the play, and according to Cargill, James was much upset. He desired to refute the American image in the play. Of course, he does just that in *The American*.

Cargill then goes on to examine the novel as "the first international novel." Cargill points out that it is not just the foreign setting that makes a novel international. In an international work, a character has the attributes of one civilization but he is placed in another civilization. There he must call on all his resources of character. The author must make sure he has not fallen into distortions and lost the individuality of the people involved.

James manages the American aspect of Newman well by emphasizing his self-confidence and easy assurance. James also adds some other traits, such as Newman's candor, which individualize his hero. James also makes his hero magnanimous. He is generous, and it is his silent judgment that is most difficult for the Bellegardes to bear. Probably, Reverend Babcock was introduced to be a contrast to Newman.

Cargill points out that James makes the Bellegardes too obvious; that is, they reveal themselves too directly. A little later in the essay, Cargill says that for those readers who are partisans of Newman, James has presented the Bellegardes with "convincing skill." He says that they are probably more convincing in their speeches to Newman than they are in action. However, James's greatest failure in the book is the fact that the reader does not get to know Claire well enough. According to Cargill, James does not prepare the reader for Claire's decision to enter a convent. James should have given some hint of her religious devotion before her final resolve. It seems as though James meant her final decision to be a check on the entire family.

Cargill also questions the crime of Madame de Bellegarde, not whether she was capable of it, but whether it was necessary to kill her husband just to marry off her daughter. Finally, says

Cargill, for all the **realism** in the details of the novel, James fell into the way of the sensationalist dramatist.

JOSEPH WARREN BEACH, "THE METHOD OF HENRY JAMES"

Still one of the best studies of the techniques and **themes** of Henry James although it was first published in 1918, this study has some good comments on *The American*. Beach points out that this is James's first treatment of a **theme** that would occupy his writing mind for a long time, the **theme** of "the contrast of the American and European cultures." *The American* has no antecedents and traditions, and he is brought into contact with a society where these things constitute their whole way of life. The American is simple, straight-forward, an easy-going westerner. The Europeans are formal, sophisticated, inordinately polite and treacherous people. Beach says that this forms the basis for a very rich and varied story. James leaves nothing out, he continues. The love affair of Valentin and Noémie Nioche is a contrast to the love affair of Newman and Claire. Beach says that nothing of the consciousness of Newman comes out in the novel. It is not a spiritual dilemma. He says there is a gallant fight for a woman, a tragic social contrast, and the hero's involvement. That is the subject of the novel, and that is why the novel is not great.

F. W. DUPEE, "HENRY JAMES"

The American is really funny, says Dupee. Probably, this is an indication of James's coming maturity and new born confidence. Dupee, earlier than these comments, points out that James's unique **theme** was "the American in contact with Europeans."

James treated this subject sometimes at length, sometimes very briefly. *The American* was the "most exuberant" of these stories. Those people who like the realistic school will of course see that both Newman and the Bellegardes are romantically drawn. Even James saw this later. *The American* differs from James's later works in degree, not in kind. Dupee says that the language of the novel begins to be important in this novel. Although Christopher Newman at first seems simple, and although it is true, as Constance Rourke has pointed out (in *American Humor*), that Newman comes from native roots in America, Dupee goes much further and says that as a character Newman combines separate strains that James was developing at this time in his career. Newman is the new social upstart, and he is the new humanity produced by America.

Dupee then examines the behavior of Christopher Newman, with his symbolic name, in the novel. Newman is not in pursuit of culture in Europe. At the end of the novel, he is just as distant from the arts as he was in the beginning. Newman really wants in Europe a perfect wife, "some supreme product of old world civilization." Of course, as the reader knows, Newman does not get Claire, even after Mrs. Tristram presents her to the hero. Newman loses her to the old world institution of the Convent, just as Valentin loses his life to the old world institution called the Duel. Newman makes a choice at the end of the novel, but he does not do so with forgiveness in his mind, as James indicates in his preface.

Dupee ends his discussion of *The American* by pointing out that James was criticized by the editor of the *Atlantic* because the novel defied realism. That editor was William Dean Howells, a famous American realistic novelist in his own right and friend of Henry James. As the reader knows, James recognized his romantic subject in his Preface.

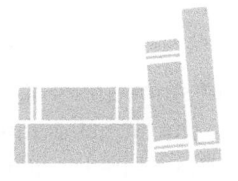

THE AMERICAN

ESSAY QUESTIONS AND ANSWERS

Question: Discuss the significance of the title of the novel, *The American*.

Answer: Henry James chose an audacious title for the novel, for *The American* commits the writer, it seems, to the examination of a national type. The developing of a type is not the sole subject of the work, however. James chose the American man, the new man, gave him the necessary attributes, and then placed him in direct contrast to a completely different way of life. What Henry James meant by "The American" was the American in relation to European life.

One can see that James was careful in his choice of his character and what he stood for. First, he chose a very successful businessman, one who had made his fortune through hard work and self-reliance, two cherished American ideals. James then made his hero a westerner, a man from the last frontier of American life. The personality of the man followed fairly easily: he was innocent, honest, direct, self-confident, and self-assured. His candor made him a man of an open and sincere nature.

Once the character traits of the American are understood, one can move to the significance of this title. James chose the name Christopher Newman. Early in the novel, Mademoiselle Nioche finds the first name droll because it is also the name of the founder of America. The American is a founder and a "new" man. He represents a new world with new and different values. He represents innocence and eagerness. And these aspects of the American come out best when Christopher Newman is placed in the center of European society, or the society of the old world, which does not tolerate any new men, or new ideas, or new thoughts. All the things that Newman represents are a threat to the established order of things as the Europeans know them.

The final significance of the title of the novel comes when the reader realizes that Henry James has made his contrast not because he has wanted to examine types of peoples, but because he has wanted to place value on his figures. At the end of the novel, when Newman chooses, because of his nature, not to reveal the secret of the Bellegardes, he proves to be the real noble figure. The Europeans possess the social graces that Newman does not, but he possesses the inner grace, as an American, that they can no longer attain.

Question: Discuss the world of the Bellegardes and what they represent.

Answer: The world of the Bellegardes is a world of antiquity. The Bellegarde family goes back to the time of Charlemagne, and the world of Madame de Bellegarde goes back to the 16th century. Age, antecedents, and the traditions that have accrued form the basis for this existence. One can see the world of the Bellegardes in the present time by the way that their house is set far back from the street and is isolated from the rest of the city. The Bellegarde château is old and musty, thinks Newman, and difficult to get to. Symbolically, one must leave his carriage and walk the final distance to the formidable edifice.

The physical world of the Bellegardes supports the society of the Bellegardes. Their society is one of dukes, counts, and barons. They engage in no useful activity, but they have their strict code of behavior. Their conversation is replete with names of people they know, and they measure each other by the length of their noble past. At the engagement party of the Bellegardes, for example, people are always introduced in order of rank, and these same people are concerned with the antecedents of a man like Newman.

But one must ask himself what all these things, which are physical, represent. The world of the Bellegardes, the world of the old aristocracy, is isolated. It lives in the past, completely divorced from the realities of the present. Although the economic status of the Bellegardes is poor and they have to combine their households, they still maintain appearances. The world of the Bellegardes is sterile, for when one of the members tries to express himself individually, as does Valentin when he is in school, he is chastized and reprimanded. The world of the Bellegardes is rigid, as one can see when Newman threatens it. The people protect themselves with treachery. The world of the Bellegardes is immoral because it tries to bend the private will of the people to the established rules of behavior and decorum. Finally, the world of the Bellegardes is evil and barren, it is corrupt. One can see all these things in Madame Dandelard who shows to all her callers the marks of the beating she has tolerated, and in the fat, comical duchess discussing the famous people she has known, with a complete and blind ignorance of the rest of the world.

Question: Explain the **climax** of the novel.

Answer: One can say that there are two climaxes in *The American*. The first is less obvious, but it is probably the more telling one. At the party that the Bellegardes have given to introduce Newman to their friends, Newman, who is ecstatically happy over the prospect of his marriage to the beautiful Claire and is becoming more confident as the evening is wearing on, finally comes to his apparent mother-in-law, Madame de Bellegarde, and asks her to accompany him in a walk through the rooms for the guests to see them. Madame de Bellegarde accepts and walks with Newman. When she reaches the final room, however, she quietly says, "That will be enough, sir," and goes to the outstretched arms of her son Urbain in an obvious show of relief. That quiet statement to Newman, one can consider the climax of the novel because it was then, as the old lady says later, that she realized that she could not allow the marriage to take place. She felt that she was humiliated before her friends. It is at this point obviously that Madame de Bellegarde makes her resolve, and there is no turning. One can consider that the climactic moment, for once Madame de Bellegarde has decided, Newman has lost his suit.

Closely linked to this scene, of course, is the scene when Newman enters the house of the Bellegardes and is told by Claire that the marriage cannot take place. One can easily see that that too is climactic in a much more direct sense. However, the final climactic moment in the novel occurs, if one remembers that the novel is primarily the study of Newman's involvement and his subsequent behavior, when Newman stands on the Rue d'Enfer and stares at the wall of the convent where now Claire is a Carmelite nun. Although he does not understand the significance of the place at all, Newman does decide the flight of his imagination is over. He is prepared then, and only then, to burn the letter that he has been carrying. He is ready to make his final act for the love of Claire. Since he was not able to get her, there is no need to worry about the existence of the Bellegardes. Although this moment is never referred to as the **climax**, it is the central point in the life of Newman.

Question: How does Newman behave once the Bellegardes have rejected him?

Answer: It would be easy, especially in the light of the facts of the ending of the novel, to think that the last part of the novel concerns the final forgiveness of the Bellegardes by Newman. That is not the case at all. From the moment that the Bellegardes shockingly reject him because he is "too commercial," Newman feels a deep hurt. He is hurt because he has lost the woman he loves, and he is hurt because his pride is badly damaged. One must not forget that Newman has been able to accomplish what he has set out to do in life. His success and his ability to overcome obstacles are important to him. At first, Newman is bent on revenge. He laughs in the churchyard once he has heard the secret of the Bellegardes from Mrs. Bread. He takes great pleasure in having the note. For example, the first time he calls at the home of his enemies, he decides not to enter the house, because he is comforted by the information he has. Newman wants desperately to hurt the mother and brother of Claire. He finally springs the note on the two by accosting them in a park. He has his momentary success when he sees Madame de Bellegarde agitated and Urbain frozen with fear, but the pleasure and the success are hollow, Newman later realizes. As Henry James points out in his preface to the novel, what causes Newman to leave the Bellegardes alone is his own sense of disgust and his magnanimous character. Newman realizes at the end that the whole thing is not worth it any longer, that no matter what he does - made clear in the apartment of the fat duchess - the world of the Bellegardes will remain as it is. These are the facts of Newman's behavior, not some ideal truths.

Question: What position does Valentin de Bellegarde have in the novel and how does James use him?

Answer: With the character of Valentin James was able to accomplish much in the novel. In the first place, Valentin is trying to break away from the family. He holds a moral grudge against the family. He is willing to help Newman, because he knows about the evil that his mother and his brother have been willing to commit. In other words, Valentin has the position of a commentator on the whole family, especially as he apologizes for what they are. James, moreover, uses Valentin to show the irony of the position of one who wants to break away from the way of life of the nobility and get a job so that he can become an individual. The irony comes out in that it is not the family that stops Valentin and kills him, but the institutions that the family stands for. It is the sense of honor and the "barbarous" institution of the duel that kill Valentin. In other words, James is saying that since Valentin was born a nobleman, he could not escape it. Valentin is an important figure in the deeper meanings of the work.

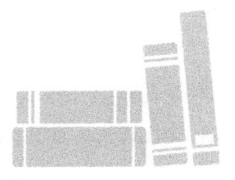

SELECTED BIBLIOGRAPHY

Henry James has been discussed at great length by the critics and the studies of his works are numerous; therefore the following should be helpful for the beginning and advanced student. Aside from the works mentioned here, there are numerous articles in magazines.

BIOGRAPHY

The three volumes of James's autobiography are edited in one volume by F. W. Dupee, *Henry James's Autobiography*, 1956. This is the best place to begin.

The outstanding biography of Henry James is written by Leon Edel, who reconstructs the life of James from all possible sources, especially from his letters. The biography will be in four volumes when it is completed. At the present three volumes have appeared: *Henry James: The Untried Years, 1843-1870*, 1953; *Henry James: The Conquest of London, 1870-1881*; and *Henry James: The Middle Years, 1882-1895*, both in 1962. The fourth volume, *The Master, 1895-1916*, is in preparation.

An excellent one volume study of James with very sound critical judgment throughout and an excellent view of James's career is F. W. Dupee's *Henry James*, 1951.

Of importance in studying James fully are his letters: *Selected Letters of Henry James*, edited by Leon Edel, 1960.

CRITICISM

All James students should begin with two edited works of James's own writings, for they contain extraordinary insight into the problems that he faced as a writer and a critic. James's methods of writing and making notes can best be seen in *The Notebooks of Henry James*, edited by F. O. Matthiessen and Kenneth Murdock, 1947. James's Prefaces are collected in a separate volume by R. P. Blackmur, who supplies an excellent introduction with an extensive analysis, *The Art of the Novel*, 1959.

All the literary histories of American literature contain chapters on Henry James, and a beginning student will do well to begin with one of these. A long chapter by R. P. Blackmur on James in the *Literary History of the United States*, 1948, gives a complete view of James.

Of the separate volumes on James, a very useful one for the student is a collection of essays edited by F. W. Dupee, *The Question of Henry James*, 1945. There are discussions and essays by different critics on most of the problems in James study.

One early study that was particularly critical of James's expatriation to Europe and questioned the whole idea of Europe because it was seen too idealistically by the later James was Van Wyck Brooks's *The Pilgrimage of Henry James*, 1925.

A short and general view of the whole subject, very valuable to the beginning student, is Edel's *Henry James*, 1960, University of Minnesota Pamphlets on American Writers.

BIBLIOGRAPHY

Almost all of the above works have useful bibliographies.

A good descriptive bibliography that organizes the criticism in order for the student is the one by Robert Spiller in *Eight American Authors: A Review of Research and Criticism*, edited by Floyd Stovall, 1956.

A much fuller and more scholarly bibliography is Leon Edel and D. H. Laurence's, *A Bibliography of Henry James*, 1958.

EXPLORE THE ENTIRE LIBRARY OF BRIGHT NOTES STUDY GUIDES

From Shakespeare to Sinclair Lewis and from Plato to Pearl S. Buck, The Bright Notes Study Guide library spans hundreds of volumes, providing clear and comprehensive insights into the world's greatest literature. Discover more, faster with the Bright Notes Study Guide to the classics you're reading today.

See the entire library of available
Bright Notes guides at **BrightNotes.com**

Available in print and digital wherever books are sold

IP INFLUENCE PUBLISHERS

www.ingramcontent.com/pod-product-compliance
Ingram Content Group UK Ltd.
Pitfield, Milton Keynes, MK11 3LW, UK
UKHW020644250325
5143UKWH00034B/430